Three Years Among the

Indians and Mexicans

KEYSTONE WESTERN AMERICANA SERIES

Archibald Hanna and William H. Goetzmann,
General Editors

Three Years Among the Indians and Mexicans

by Thomas James

The 1846 Edition, Unabridged

Introduction by A. P. Nasatir

J. B. LIPPINCOTT COMPANY
Philadelphia and New York

INTRODUCTION

STUDENTS AND READERS who seek excitement, wild adventure, or just good reading usually resort to novels, to *True Adventure*, to the dignified *Saturday Evening Post*, or to the venerable *Blue Book*. But better stories—and far closer to the truth in their depiction of life in the American West in the time of mountain men, pathfinders, travelers, and Indians—are the true narratives of fur traders and trappers of the savage country of the Upper Missouri after Lewis and Clark returned from their great adventure in 1806. Indeed, if the traders and trappers had been literary men, and if all had written their own narratives, there would be no reason to read of such matters in novels.

Few of the plain, ordinary men of the West wrote down their stories, however. Hence, when a man who participated in those events, who suffered many hair's-breadth escapes, and who acquired a very considerable fund of information about Indian and Mexican customs at a critical period—when such a man writes his narrative with "literary excellence," then he must command the attention of both readers and students. Such a work is General Thomas James's *Three Years Among the Indians and Mexicans*. Moreover, this work merits attention because James supplies much historical information about events on which there are no primary sources other than his narrative. This applies both to James's adventures as a member of the St. Louis Missouri Fur Company's expedition to the headwaters of the Missouri River in 1809 and 1810, and to his narrative of his trading ventures, in 1821–1824, across the Great Plains to Santa Fé, and among the Comanches. There are other narratives of the Southwest, contemporaneous with James's, which round out the story of the first Americans to reach Santa Fé from Missouri—the story, as I choose to call it, of "The Genesis of the Santa Fé Trail."

General James used to delight in telling and retelling his adventures. No doubt those stories changed with repetition, but out of them, and perhaps at the urging of friends who had heard his tales, James wrote *Three Years Among the Indians and Mexicans,* hoping, he said, to awaken his countrymen to the importance of peaceful and friendly relations with the powerful Comanches. The student of history must temper his reliance upon James's book as a fundamental historical source, because, among other reasons, it is a narrative dictated and published many years after the events it describes. It is the dismay of the historian that James actually kept a journal on his trip to the Southwest, but that, sad to say, one of his trunks containing his journal fell into the river, and, some "rhubarb dissolving became mixed with my shirts, journal, invoice and other papers," thereby rendering them completely useless—ruining the journal. The General, at the time of the telling, says: "My memory which has always been very retentive of events and incidents, enables me to supply this loss with sufficient accuracy." Indeed, he had a very good memory—but old age does play tricks with one's recollections. James is not always completely accurate, and interesting and important as his story is, there are details that do not measure up to historical standards.

An editor of one edition of James's book stated, and most historians have believed, that James's account of the 1809–1810 trip up the Missouri was the only source for that expedition of Manuel Lisa and his men, but I have found a portion of another account, by a Dr. Thomas, who was in the boat where James himself was the steersman or "captain," which is reproduced here as Appendix A. (Dr. Thomas's account appeared in the *Louisiana Gazette* and ran in more than one issue, but unfortunately I can find only the first installment.)

James's *Three Years* was not published until 1846, but in 1834—ten years after his return from the Southwest, and twelve years before he wrote the book—he very briefly summarized most of the story in a letter to President Jackson to ask for a position or agency among the Comanches. This letter, which I owe to the kindness of Professor Covington, who discovered it in the National Archives, is given here as Appendix B.

General Thomas James, author of *Three Years Among the Indians and Mexicans,* was born in Maryland November 4, 1782, son of Joseph Austin and Elizabeth Hosten James. Some years later, his parents moved to Kentucky, where Thomas's brother, James A. James, was born in 1798. About 1803 the family moved to the American Bottom of southern Illinois. From there James accompanied his father to Florissant, near St. Louis, where the elder James acquired a strip of land on the common which now forms a portion of the Seminary farm; on February 16, 1814, the father and two of his sons, including Thomas, signed a record of the parishioners endorsing a new code of parochial regulations.

Thomas James was living at Florissant in 1806 when Lewis and Clark returned from their famous expedition, bringing with them some Indian chiefs to visit Washington. Their return triggered a rush of American traders and trappers into the Upper Missouri country, one of whom was Manuel Lisa, who ascended the river in 1807. The United States Army failed to return the Mandan Chief Shehaka to his home in 1807 because of Arikara hostility, and when the St. Louis Missouri Fur Company was formed in 1809, one of its first missions was the return of Shehaka to his home, under contract with the government. The military section of the expedition was headed by the veteran Indian trader and agent Pierre Chouteau, but once the mission of seeing Shehaka safely home had been fulfilled, it was (with the exception of the military) to be a private trading expedition led by Manuel Lisa in the name of the St. Louis Missouri Fur Company.

Thomas James, already a seasoned frontiersman, enlisted, and signed a three-year contract with the Company, under which document he was to labor and assist in transporting, trapping, hunting, and collecting meats and furs. The Company was to furnish to him four men and equipment when they should reach the headwaters of the Missouri, and they were to divide the proceeds into fifths. The duration of the contract was for three years unless he should be discharged by the Company, and a penalty of $500 was provided if either party should break the contract; the agreement was signed in St. Louis on March 29, 1809.

Thomas James ascended the Missouri with the expedition. He was quarrelsome, and soon became bitter; he did not spare any person who incurred his dislike, and among these was Manuel Lisa, with whom he quarreled. He quit the Company, but later, at Fort Ramón, he joined Ménard and Henry's detachment for the first organized invasion of the hostile Blackfeet area, and returned to St. Louis with Ménard in August,

1810. The story of his troubles on the Upper Missouri is told in the first two chapters of his book, but it appears that some of the trouble arose from the fact that the Americans on the trip were in reality private adventurers, each out on his own account, each concerned more with what he wanted—a chance to reach the trapping grounds—than with the long-established customs of such expeditions. The Company had agreed to furnish the men with subsistence until they should reach the hunting and trapping grounds, and the men were to help navigate and equip the boats.

Back in St. Louis in 1810, James tells us that more than a year on the Upper Missouri had put him $200 in debt, and he blamed Lisa for it. He was also in debt to John Colter and others. In September, 1810, William Clark on behalf of the Company sued James on a note for $249.81; James sued the Company for $750 for breach of contract. At the trial, James could not find his witnesses, and the case was dismissed. In October, 1814, the Company again sued James, but the records show no judgment; the suit seems to have been settled by James's giving the Company a note for $100. In the same month, the administrators of Colter's estate sued James for $140 on his note of October 7, 1809, but the case was settled without trial.

In the fall of 1810 James went to Pennsylvania, where he stayed about two years and where he married. He returned to St. Louis in the fall of 1813, obtained a keelboat and entered the business of conveying goods between Pittsburgh and St. Louis.

In 1815 he took a stock of goods from McKnight and Brady, and opened a store at Harrisonville, Illinois. John McKnight, a Virginia man, had come to St. Louis in April, 1809, with Thomas Brady. Together they built up a large mercantile business in St. Louis, bought property in Missouri and Illinois, especially in East St. Louis and in Harrisonville, in the American Bottom in Monroe County, Illinois, about thirty miles from St. Louis; and James's store was a branch of the McKnight and Brady business.

In 1812, James Baird, Samuel Chambers, and Robert McKnight (a brother of John), had bought goods from McKnight and Brady and gone to Santa Fé, where they were arrested by Spanish authorities. They were imprisoned in Chihuahua, and some of them were released in 1820—but not Robert McKnight.

In the meantime, in 1818, James had gone to Baltimore and bought $17,000 worth of goods, on which he lost a great deal of money; in fact he was on the verge of bankruptcy when he teamed up with John McKnight to take $10,000 worth of goods to Santa Fé. They left in a keelboat in May, 1821, with a following of young and daring men, descended the Mississippi and went up the Arkansas and the North Fork of the Canadian. The party underwent extreme hardships and many perils, and under duress gave away much of their goods to the Comanches.

They met the Glenn-Fowler party which refused to join up with their party and James developed an extreme dislike for Glenn. James arrived in Santa Fé on December 1, 1821, and says he was the first American trader to reach Santa Fé after the Mexican revolution. He seems to be mistaken, however, for Becknell had preceded him by about two weeks. It is extremely odd that James never mentions Becknell, and Becknell does not mention James. It was hardly possible in those days for two Americans to be in Santa Fé and in Taos without at least knowing about each other.

In Santa Fé, James did trade his merchandise, but at a considerable net loss because of the goods he had given to the Indians. Robert McKnight went to Durango and obtained the release of his brother, and James and the McKnights returned to St. Louis in mid-July, 1822, having frequently been within hailing distance of the Glenn-Fowler party. In St. Louis James discovered that he had been presumed dead. Later that year, he and the two McKnights took a trading party into the Comanche country, and after many disasters, including the death of John McKnight, the party returned in 1824. That trip, made in still another effort to recoup his fortune, is related by James in his last two chapters; again he lost his property, which he probably had obtained on credit on the strength of McKnight's financial standing.

Bereft of fortune but not of honor, James then resigned himself to a life of poverty and to the humdrum of a more settled existence, to his family, and to payment of his debts. He had brought $2,500 from Santa Fé (out of his original $10,000 or $12,000), and he gave up all his property, and operated a mill and distillery at what came to be known as James's Mill, later Monroe City. He was not making enough to pay his debts, and Robert McKnight tried to get a lucrative position in the mines for him, but was unsuccessful. During those long years of defeat and hardships, James's brother supported his family and provided for the education of his children; it was all James could do to pay off his debts and leave his heirs only "a good example and an unsullied name."

Thomas James must have been liked by his neighbors, for he was honored on many occasions. In 1825 he was elected General of the Second Brigade, First Division, Illinois militia, and in the same year he was elected to represent Monroe County in the state legislature, where he served two years. In 1827 he was appointed postmaster, and held that office until his death. He served as a major in the Black Hawk War, and commanded a "spy" battalion. In 1839, with his brother James, he was agent for the lottery drawing at Harrisonville; and he was appointed to receive subscriptions for the State Bank of Kaskaskia.

He tried, as I have mentioned, to get an appointment from President Jackson as agent to the Comanches, in the hope that those Indians would remunerate him for the goods which they despoiled him of earlier, but in spite of support from his fellow citizens was unsuccessful. He is said to have practiced medicine, and his son became a well-known physician. James died intestate in Monroe County December 17, 1847, and he and his wife are buried in the old Catholic cemetery at Madonnaville, a short distance from Monroe City. Some members of his family are still living, and James's Lick, near Florissant, is named for the James family.

One year before his death, *Three Years Among the Indians and Mexicans* was published by the *War Eagle*, a weekly newspaper edited by Elam Rust at Waterloo, Illinois. The book has literary quality, and since Thomas James did not have much formal education, it has been discovered that he dictated his exciting narrative to Nathaniel Niles, who probably also did the writing. Niles was born in Plainfield, New York, in 1817, and studied law in New York City; about 1840 he migrated to Belleville, Illinois, where he taught school, practiced law and politics, edited a newspaper, served in the Black Hawk and Civil Wars, was in the state legislature, was county judge and a devotee of literature. The book was attacked immediately after publication—probably because of James's disparaging remarks about many persons still living at that time—and Niles gathered as many copies as he could, and destroyed them; the original edition is now very rare. Judge Walter B. Douglas used one of the few copies in existence for his articles on Manuel Lisa; later he reprinted the James book with notes and appendices, which has made his edition a real contribution to historical researchers. Unfortunately, however, that printing by the Missouri Historical Society was limited, and even that edition now brings a hundred dollars. In 1953, the Lakeside Classics reprinted the James book, with editing by Milo Quaife, who corrected some of the crudities and replaced the chapter summaries with simple titles. Since the James book has been hard to acquire and has been little used by historians of the West, an inexpensive reissue of the original edition, published at a price to make it easily available and cheap enough for students, should be a distinct benefit to historians.

Thomas James was six feet tall, muscular, intelligent, and outspoken; he was a man of bitter prejudices and disparaged those who ill-treated him and those with whom he quarreled. He made ominous statements against Lisa and the partners of the St. Louis Missouri Fur Company, made derisive comments about Hugh Glenn, and pictured missionaries as undesirable citizens. But his attitude toward the Indians, from whom he suffered so much, is in surprising contrast to his feeling about the whites. Of Americans, John McKnight is the only one of whom he speaks in terms of affection; for the Indians, James exhibits kindness, liking, and admiration.

James's book, though written some twenty-five years after the events it narrates, and distorted by its author's highly critical views, is, despite these two serious limitations, and despite the fact that it is sometimes faulty as to both dates and facts, one of the most fascinating first-hand records of early experiences on the Far Western frontier, and invaluable for its information regarding episodes and persons either ignored or slighted by other writers. *Three Years Among the Indians and Mexicans* is a most important contribution to the literature of the West.

A. P. NASATIR

San Diego State College
November 16, 1961

CONTENTS

CHAPTER I   1

Introduction—Missouri Fur Company—Terms of Engagement with them—Departure for the Trapping Grounds—Incidents on the Route—The Pork Meeting—Scenery—Check—A Western Pioneer—His affair with the Irishman—A Hunting Excursion—The Rickarees—The Mandans—The Gros Ventres—The Company's Fort—Cheek and Ried—Friends between the French and Americans—Violation of Contract by Company—Departure for Upper Missouri—Wintering—Trip across the Country—Famine and Cold—Scenery on the Yellow Stone—Manuel's Fort—Col. Menard and Manuel Liza—Indian Murders—A Snow Storm in the Mountains—Blindness—Arrival at the Forks of the Missouri —Preparations for business.

CHAPTER II   29

Colter's Race and escapes—Separation for trapping—Descent of the Missouri—A fine Landscape—Bad luck—Alarm from Indians —Retreat to the Fort—Death of Cheek—Pursuit of the Indians —Return—The White Bears—Incidents of hunting—Return to the Twenty Five Yard river—A party of Gros Ventres—Suspected Robbery—Interview with the Crows—Rapid crossing of the Yellow Stone—Descent to the Fort and the *"Cache"*—Robbery made certain—Passage to the Missouri—Indian character and customs—A Spree, ending almost tragically—Generosity of the Company—Settlement with them—A sage reflection.

CHAPTER III   57

Employment from 1810 to 1821—The First Santa Fe Traders—Members of the Fourth Santa Fe expedition—Ascent of the Arkansas—Vaugean—Removal of the Town of Little Rock—Fort Smith and Major Bradford—Trading with the Osages—Capt. Prior—Salt River—Salt Plains and Shining Mountains—Robbery by the Indians—Sufferings from thirst—Attack by the Indians—Further Robberies—The One Eyed Chief and Big Star—Indian Council—Critical Situation—Rescue by Spanish officers—Cordaro Journey continued—San Miguil Peccas and its Indian inhabitants—Santa Fe—Farming.

CHAPTER IV   84

Interview with Governor Malgaris—Commencement of business
—Departure of McKnight—Arrival of Cordaro—His Speech—His
visit to Nacotoche—His death and character—Hugh Glenn—
Celebration of Mexican Independence—Gambling and dissipation—Mexican Indians—Domestic manufactures—Visit of the
Utahs—Their Horses—Speech of the Chief Lechat—War with
the Navahoes—Cowardly murder of their Chiefs by the Spaniards—Militia of Santa Fe—Attempt to go to Senoria—Stopped
by the Governor—Interview with the Adjutant—Selling out—
Hugh Glenn again—How the Governor paid me a Debt—Spanish
Justice—Departure for home.

CHAPTER V   103

Col. Glenn's conversion—His profits thereby—Avenues to New
Mexico—An instance of Spanish treachery and cruelty—Glenn's
cowardice—Meeting with the Pawnee—Mexican Indians—Battle
between the Pawnees and Osages—Disappearance of Glenn—
Chouteau and the Osages—Indian revenge—Passage of the
Shoshoua—Singular Ferrying—Entrance into Missouri—Robbery
by the Osages—Interview with Missionaries—Arrival at St. Louis
—More of Glenn—Home—Still greater troubles with creditors
than with the Indians.

CHAPTER VI   123

Endeavors to get out of debt—Proposition of John McKnight—
Preparations for another expedition—Journey to the Arkansas—
Ascent of the Canadian and North Fork—Hunting Bears, Elks,
&c.—Fort commenced—Conversation with McKnight and his
departure in search of Camanches—Continued ascent of the
Canadian North Fork—A new Fort—Return of Potter and Ivy—
Robert McKnight goes out in search of his brother—He returns
with Indians—Charges them with the murder of his brother—I
go out to the Camanche village—Incidents there—A council—
The One Eyed Chief—The whole band start for the Fort—A
guard placed over me—Encampment—The One Eyed adopts me
as his brother—He changes my relations with his tribes—Catching wild horses—Arrival at the Fort—Fright of some "brave"
men—Trade—A robbery—The One Eyed punishes the thieves—
Fate of John McKnight—Mourning stopped—Indian customs—
A dance—A case of arbitration by the One Eyed—Indian horsemanship—Parting with the Chiefs—Conversation with Alsarea—
The horse Checoba—A Bucephalus.

CHAPTER VII   152

We start for home—A *stampedo*—Loss of a hundred horses—
Interview with a Chief and his tribe—Pursued by Indians—Passage through the Cross Timbers—Death of horses by flies—Night
travelling—Arrival at the Arkansas—Death of hoses by the
Feresy—Loss of skins and robes by embezzlement—Start for
home—Breakfast with a Cherokee Chief—James Rogers—An old
Cherokee—Interview with Missionaries—Arrival at home—Troubles from debt—An emergence at last—Conclusion.

Appendices:

A. Journal of a Voyage from St. Louis, La., to the Mandan
    Village, by Doctor Thomas (1809)   167
B. Letter of Thomas James to President Andrew Jackson,
    February 21, 1834   170

MAPS

General James' Upper Missouri River Expedition of 1809-
    1810   *facing* p. 1
Southwestern Expeditions of General James   56

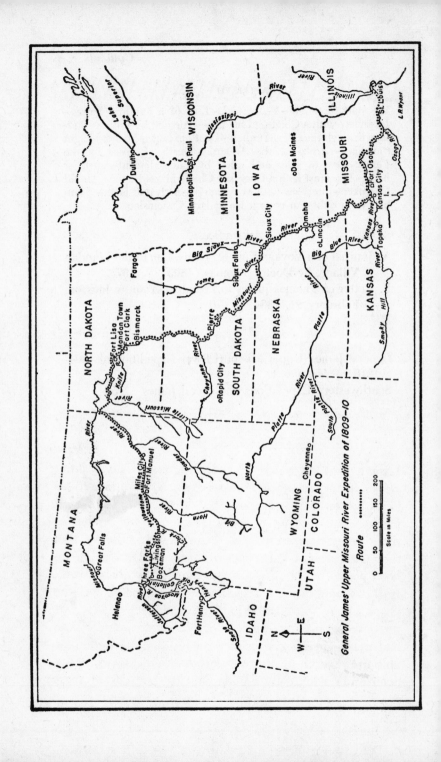

Three Years Among the

Indians and Mexicans

CHAPTER I

Introduction—Missouri Fur Company—Terms of Engagement with them—Departure for the Trapping Grounds—Incidents on the Route—The Pork Meeting—Scenery—Check—A Western Pioneer—His affair with the Irishman—A Hunting Excursion—The Rickarees—The Mandans—The Gros Ventres—The Company's Fort—Cheek and Ried—Friends between the French and Americans—Violation of Contract by Company—Departure for Upper Missouri—Wintering—Trip across the Country—Famine and Cold—Scenery on the Yellow Stone—Manuel's Fort—Col. Menard and Manuel Liza—Indian Murders—A Snow Storm in the Mountains—Blindness—Arrival at the Forks of the Missouri—Preparations for business.

I HAVE OFTEN amused myself and friends, by relating stories of my adventures in the West, and am led to believe, by the, perhaps, too partial representations of those friends, that my life in the Prairies and Mountains for three years, is worthy of a record more enduring than their memories. I have passed a year and a half on the head waters of the Missouri and among the gorges of the Rocky Mountains, as a hunter and a trapper, and two years among the Spaniards and Camanches. I have suffered much from the inclemency of nature and of man, had many "hair breadth 'scapes" and acquired considerable information illustrative of Indian and Mexican character and customs. By a plain, unvarnished tale of West-

1

ern life, of perils and of hardships, I hope to amuse the
reader who delights in accounts of wild adventure,
though found out of the pages of a novel and possessing
no attraction but their unadorned truthfulness. I am now
on the shady side of sixty, with mind and memory unim-
paired. If my reminiscenses, as recorded in the following
pages, serve to awaken my countrymen of the West and
South-west, now thank God, including Texas, to the importance of peaceful and friendly relations with the most
powerful tribe of Indians on the continent, the Camanches, I shall not regard the labor of preparing these sheets
as bestowed in vain.

In the year 1803, when twenty-two years of age, I
emigrated with my father from Kentucky to Illinois. In
the spring of 1807 we removed from Illinois to Missouri,
which were then, both Territories, and settled in the town
of St. Ferdinand, near St. Louis. In the fall of this year,
Lewis and Clark returned from Oregon and the Pacific
Ocean, whither they had been sent by the administration of Jefferson in the first exploring expedition west of
the Rocky Mountains, and their accounts of that wild
region, with those of their companions, first excited a
spirit of trafficking adventure among the young men of
the West. They had brought with them from the Upper
Missouri, a Chief named Shehaka, of the Mandan tribe of
Indians. This Chief, in company with Lewis and Clark
visited the "Great Father" at Washington City, and returned to St. Louis in the following Spring (1808) with
Lewis, who, in the mean time had been appointed Governor of Missouri Territory. He sent the Chief Shehaka up
the Missouri with an escort of about forty United States
troops, under Capt. Prior. On their arrival in the country
of the Rickarees, a warlike tribe, next East or this side
of the Mandans, they were attacked by the former tribe,
and eight or ten soldiers killed. This event so disheartened

the rest, that they returned with Shehaka to St. Louis. The Missouri Fur Company had just been formed, and they projected an expedition up the Missouri and to the Rocky Mountains, which was to start in the spring of the following year, 1809. The company consisted of ten partners, among whom was M. Gratiot, Pierre Menard, Sam'l. Morrison, Pierrie Chouteau, Manuel Liza, Major Henry, M. L'Abbadeau and Reuben Lewis. Gov. Lewis was also said to have had an interest in the concern. The company contracted with him to convey the Mandan Chief to his tribe, for the sum, as I was informed of $10,000. I enlisted in this expedition, which was raised for trading with the Indians and trapping for beaver on the head waters of the Missouri and Columbia rivers. The whole party, at starting, consisted of 350 men, of whom about one half were Americans and the remainder Canadian Frenchmen and Creoles of Kaskaskia, St. Louis and other places. The French were all veteran *voyageurs,* thoroughly inured to boating and trapping. Manuel Liza, called by the men "Esaw" had enlisted many of them in Detroit for this expedition, and hired them by the year. We Americans were all private adventurers, each on his own hook, and were led into the enterprise by the promises of the company, who agreed to subsist us to the trapping grounds, we helping to navigate the boats, and on our arrival there they were to furnish us each with a rifle and sufficient ammunition, six good beaver traps and also four men of their hired French, to be under our individual commands for a period of three years. By the terms of the contract each of us was to divide one-fourth of the profits of our joint labor with the four men thus to be appointed to us. How we were deceived and taken in, will be seen in the sequel. The "company" made us the fairest promises in St. Louis, only to break them in the Indian country. Liza, or Esaw, or Manuel as he was variously called, had the principal command. He was a Spaniard or Mexican by birth, and bore a very bad reputation in the country and among the Americans. He had been on the head waters of the Missouri, the year before with a company of about fifty men and had met with great success in catching beaver and trading with the Indians. He had built a Fort, called "Manuel's Fort" at the junction or fork of the Big Horn and Yellow Stone rivers, and left a garrison of hunters in it when he returned in the Spring of this year, and went into the Missouri Fur Company. He was suspected of having invited the Rickarees to attack the Government troops under Capt. Prior, with Shehaka the year before, for the purpose of preventing the traders and trappers who were with the troops from getting into the upper country. Mr. Choteau and Col. Menard acted jointly with Liza in conducting the expedition. I went as steersman or "captain" of one of the barges, with about twenty-four men, all Americans, under my command. There were thirteen barges and keel boats in all. On my barge I had Doct. Thomas, the surgeon of the company, and Reuben Lewis, brother of Merryweather Lewis, the Governor.

We started from St. Louis in the month of June, A. D. 1809, and ascended the Missouri by rowing, pushing with poles, *cordeling*, or pulling with ropes, warping, and sailing. My crew were light hearted, jovial men, with no care or anxiety for the future, and little fear of any danger. In the morning we regularly started by day break and stopped, generally, late at night. The partners or *bourgoises*, as the French called them, were in the forward barge, with a strong crew of hardy and skilful *voyageurs*, and there Liza and some of his colleagues lorded it over the poor fellows most arrogantly, and made them work as if their lives depended on their getting forward, with the greatest possible speed. They peremptorily required all the boats to stop in company for the night, and our barge being large and heavily loaded, the crew frequently had great difficulty in overtaking them in the evening. We occasionally had races with some of the forward barges, in which my crew of Americans proved themselves equal in a short race to their more experienced French competitors. We thus continued, with nothing of interest occurring till we passed the Platte. Six weeks of hard labor on our part, had been spent, when our allotted provisions gave out and we were compelled to live on boiled corn, without salt. At the same time all the other boats were well supplied and the gentlemen proprietors in the leading barge were faring in the most sumptuous and luxurious manner. The French hands were much better treated on all occasions than the Americans. The former were employed for a long period at stated wages and were accustomed to such service and such men as those in command of them, while we were private adventurers for our own benefit, as well as that of the company, who regarded us with suspicion and distrust. Many Americans on the passage up the river, disgusted with the treatment they received, fell off in small companies and went back. At Cote Sans Desans, opposite the mouth of the Osage, most of them returned. On reaching the Mandan country we numbered about ten Americans, having started from St. Louis with about one hundred and seventy-five and an equal number of French. After passing the Platte river my crew were worn down with hard labor and bad fare. Their boiled corn without salt or meat, did not sustain them under the fatigue of navigating the barge and the contrast between their treatment and that of the French enraged them. A meeting was the result. The company had, on our barge, thirty barrels of pork, and one morning my crew came to me in a body demanding some of these provisions. I commanded them not to break into the pork without permission, and promised, if they would work and keep up till noon, to procure some for dinner. At noon when we stopped, the men rolled up a barrel of pork on to the deck and one of them, named Cheek bestrided with a tomahawk, crying out "give the word Captain." I forbade them, as before, and went ashore to find Lewis, who had left the boat at the beginning of trouble. He said the pork was the company's and told me not to touch it. I said the men would and should have some of it, and went back to the boat to give the "word" to Cheek. Lewis hastened to the *"bourgeoise"* in their barge close by, to give the alarm. I could see them in their cabin, from the shore where I stood, playing cards and drinking. Lewis entered with the news that "James' crew were taking the provisions." Manuel Liza seized his pistols and ran out followed by the other partners. "What the devil, said he to me, is the matter with you and your men?" We are starving, said I, and we must have something better than boiled corn. At the same time Cheek was brandishing his tomahawk over the pork barrel and clamoring for the "word." "Shall I break it open Captain, speak the word," he cried, while the rest of my crew were drawn up in line on the boat, with rifles, ready for action. The gentlemen *bourgeoise*, yielded before this determined array, and gave us a large supply of pork; that is, as much as we pleased to take. A few days after this we stopped to clean out the barges and the pork in ours was removed to another and its place supplied with lead. The Cheek who figured as ring-leader on this occasion was a Tennesseean, about six feet high and well proportioned. His courage was equal to any enterprise, and his rashness and headstrong obstinacy at last, in the Indian country, cost him his life. I had on my barge a large, lazy, and very impertinent Irishman, who was frequently very sulky and remiss in his duties. I was compelled one day, to call him by name for not working at the oars, saying to him he was not rowing the weight of his head. The heighth of disgrace among boatsmen is, to be publicly named by the Captain. The Irishman took my treatment in very ill humour and swore he would have satisfaction for the insult. When the boat stopped for breakfast, the men dispersed as usual, to get wood, and with them went Cheek and my friend, the Irishman. Cheek returned without him and informed me, he had whipped him "for saucing the captain." I said, Cheek I can attend to my own fighting without your assistance, or any other man's. "No by G—d said he, my Captain shan't fight while I am about." The Irishman returned, at length, to the boat, but was so badly hurt as to be unable to work for several days.

The scenery of the Upper Missouri is so familiar to the world as to render any particular description unnecessary. As you ascend the river, the woods diminish in number and extent. Beyond Council Bluffs, about 700 miles above the mouth they entirely disappear, except on the river bottoms, which are heavily timbered. The Prairies were covered with a short thick grass, about three or four inches high. At this time the game was very abundant. We saw Elk and Buffalo in vast numbers, and killed many of them. Prairie dogs and wolves were also very numerous. The Indians have thinned off the game since that time, so much that their own subsistence is frequently very scanty, and they are often in danger of starvation. Their range for hunting now extends far down into the Camanche country and Texas, and the buffalo, their only game of importance, are fast disappearing. When these valuable animals are all gone, when they are extinct on the West as they are on the East side of the Mississippi, then will the Indian race, the aboriginals of that vast region, be near their own extinction and oblivion. They cannot survive the game and with it will disappear.

The Western declivity of the Mississippi valley from the mountains to the "Father of Waters" is nearly all one great plain, with occasional rocky elevations. We saw hills at the foot of which were large heaps of pumice stone, which had the appearance of having been crumbled off from above by the action of fire. The scenery of Illinois or Missouri is a fair example of that of the whole country West to the mountains. The Prairies here, however, are vaster and more desolate. One extensive plain is usually presented to the eye of the traveller, and stretches to the horizon, without a hill, mound, tree or shrub to arrest the sight.

We continued our ascent of the river without any occurrence of importance. Below Council Bluffs we met Capt. Crooks, agent for John J. Astor, and who was trading with the Mohaws. Here all the few Americans remaining, with myself, were on the point of returning. By the solicitations and promises of the company we were induced to continue with them.

The first Indians we saw were a party of Mohaws hunting; with them were two Sioux Chiefs. They sent forward a runner to their village above and themselves came on board our boats. We found the village at the mouth of the Jaques river, perhaps twelve hundred miles, by its course, from the mouth of the Missouri. They were of the Teton tribe, which is kindred with the Sioux. As we approached the bank, which was lined with hundreds; they fired into the water before the forward barge, and as we landed, they retreated with great rapidity, making a startling noise with whistles and rattles. After landing and making fast the boats, about fifty savages took charge of them, as a guard. They wore raven feathers on the head. Their bodies were naked, save about the middle, and painted entirely black. They presented on the whole a most martial and warlike appearance in their savage mode, and performed their office of guarding the boats so well that not even a Chief was allowed to go onto them. Other Indians came with buffalo skins to be used as pulanquins or litters for carrying the partners to their council house; each was taken up and carried off in state. I was compelled by some Indians to go in the same style to the place of council. Here was a large company of old men awaiting us, and for dinner we had served up a great feast of dog's meat—a great delicacy with the Indians. The rich repast was served in forty-one wooden bowls, as I counted them, and from each bowl a dog's foot was hanging out, evidently to prove that this rarity was not a sham but a reality. Not feeling very desirous of eating of this particular dainty, I stole out and was pulled by a young Indian and invited to his wigwam. I went and partook with him of buffalo meat. We stayed with these hospitable savages two days. On arriving, we found the British flag flying, but easily persuaded them to haul it down. The Hudson's Bay Company had had their emisaries among them and were then dealing with them precisely as they are now dealing with the savages in our territory of Oregon—namely: buying them up with presents and promises, and persuading them to act as allies of Britain, in any future war with the United States. On the third day we left the friendly Tetons and proceeded up the river as before. Capt. Choteau had conceived a prejudice against Cheek, and on one occasion, ordered him to leave the boats. Lewis conveyed the order to me. I remonstrated against the cruelty of sending a man adrift in a wilderness, 1400 miles from home. He insisted, and Cheek took his gun as if he was going to obey. Lewis ordered him to leave the gun behind, which he refused to do. Lewis then commanded me to take it from him. I replied, that he or Choteau might do that themselves. The men of my boat flew to their arms, and avowed their determination of defending Cheek and sharing his fate. The order was not pursued any further. Such recontres and difficulties between the Americans and the partners, embittered their hands against us, and ultimately did us no good. Much of the ill treatment we afterwards received from them, was probably owing to the reckless assertion of our independence on every occasion and at every difficulty that occurred. After leaving the Teton village, our boat again failed of provisions, and by request of Lewis I went ashore on the North bank with one of our best hunters, named Brown, to kill some game. We went up the river, and in the evening, killed an elk, brought it to the river bank, and waited there for the boats till morning. They came up on the opposite shore and sent over a canoe to take us and our game across. The wind rose in the mean time, and blew so strong as to raise the waves very high, and render it dangerous for us all to cross together in the same canoe. We sent over the game and Brown and myself continued our course, afoot, expecting to get aboard when the boats crossed at some one of the river bends. By the middle of the day the wind had risen so high that the boats with sails hoisted, quickly went out of sight. We travelled on till evening, and struck a large bayou, which we could not cross, and took the backward course till we encamped within a mile of the spot where we had stayed the night before. The next morning we struck off from the river into the prairie, and took the best course we could, to reach the boats. Seven days elapsed, however, before we overtook them. The wind blew a strong breeze, and drove the boats along very rapidly. We killed another elk and some small game, which subsisted us till the fifth day, when our amunition gave out. Our moccasins being worn out, fell off and our feet were perfectly cut up by the prickly pear, which abounds on these prairies. At last, nearly famished and worn down, sore, lame and exhausted, we found the boats. My crew had, in vain, requested leave to wait for us, and we might have perished before the *bourgeoise* would have slackened their speed in the least, on our account. We had a narrow escape from starvation in this excursion and I was ever afterwards careful to have plenty of amunition with me when I went out—as I frequently did—on similar expeditions.

In two days after this event, we arrived at the country of the Rickarees. On approaching their village, we took precautions against an attack. A guard marched along the shore, opposite to the boats, well armed. My crew composed a part of this force. When within half a mile of the village we drew up the cannon and prepared to encamp. The whole village came out in a body, as it seemed, to met us. They had not come far toward us when an old chief rode out at full speed and with violent gestures and exclamations, warned and motioned back his countrymen from before our cannon. The event of the year before was fresh in his recollection. He supposed we were about to inflict a proper and deserved punishment for the attack on Capt. Prior's troops and the murder of eight or ten of them, the year before. This old chief drove back all who were coming out to meet us. Choteau then sent for the chief to come down to his camp and hold a council. They refused to comply with this request and appeared very suspicious of our designs. After further negotiation, they agreed to come to us and hold a council if the company's force would lay aside their arms and turn the cannon in the opposite direction. This was agreed to by the company, with the provision that a guard should be on the ground, armed, during the conference. The council was held, and Choteau harangued them on the crime committed against the government the year before. They promised better conduct for the future, but made no reparation or apology even, for the past.

In a few days we started forward through a country marked by the same general features as that described before. Thousands of buffaloe cover the prairies on both sides of the river, making them black as far as the eye could reach. In ten or twelve days the boats reached the Mandan village, where I was awaiting them. I had sallied out five days before in a hunting excursion, and arrived at the village of the Mandans in advance of the boats. These are a poor, thieving, spiritless tribe, tributary to the Gros-Ventres, who inhabit the country above them on the river. The village is on the north side of the river. The boats came up on the opposite shore. The wind, as they arrived, blew a hurricane and lashed the waves to a prodigious height. The Indians saw their chief, Shehaka, on our boats, and were almost frantic with joy and eagerness to speak with him. They have a round canoe made of hoops fastened together and a buffalo's skin stretched over them, very light and portable. With these they rowed themselves across the turbulent river, one moment lost from view between the waves, and the next, riding over them like corks. In these tubs of canoes they crossed the stream to our boats. The natives made a jubilee and celebration for the return of Shehaka and neglected every thing and every body else. They hardly saw or took the least notice of their white visitors. The partners distributed the presents sent by the government and we then made haste to leave this boorish inhospitable tribe. We ascended the Missouri to the village of the Gros-Ventres, on the south side of the river, fifteen miles above that of the Mandans. Here we found a far different race from the last; a manly, warlike and independent tribe, who might well be called for their daring and enterprising qualities, the Gros-coeurs or big-hearts instead of big-bellies. Here was our place of stopping for a short time, and of preparation for the business which had brought us hither. On our arrival at their village, four or five agents of the Hudson's Bay Company were among them, but immediately crossed the river with their goods, and bore off to the north east. We suspected them of inciting the Black Feet against us and many of our company attributed our subsequent misfortunes to their hostility. We afterwards heard that a large army of these Indians were encamped at the falls above. They traded regularly with the British traders and procured of them their arms and amunition. We built a fort near the Gros-Ventre village, and unloaded all the larger boats for the purpose of sending them back to the settlements. Having now arrived at our destination and being near the beaver region, we, the Americans, ten in number, requested the partners to furnish out traps, amunition, guns and men, according to contract. But this, they seemed to have forgotten entirely, or intended never to fulfil. We found ourselves taken in, cheated chizzled, gulled and swindled in a style that has not, perhaps, been excelled by Yankees or French, or men of any other nation, at any time in the thirty-six years that have passed over my head since this feat was performed. A stock of old and worthless traps had been brought up the river, apparently to be put off on the Americans. They offered us these traps, which we refused to take. They then endeavored to deprive us of the arms and amunition belonging to them, in our possession, and they succeeded in getting from most of us all the guns and powder of theirs that we had. Mine were taken from me with the others, by order of the partners. I do not know that all of them consented to this nefarious proceeding; I hope and should have expected that several of them would not sanction such conduct. But I heard of no protest or opposition to the acts of the majority, who behaved toward us with a want of principle and of honor that would shame most gentleman robbers of the highway.

They seemed determined to turn us out on the prairie and among the Indians, without arms, provisions or amunition. Our situation in that event, would have nearly realized the one implied in the popular expression "a cat in hell without claws." We were kept waiting two or three weeks without employment or any provisions, except what we purchased at most exhorbitant prices. We bought goods, knives, &c. of the company, on credit, and sold them to the Indians for provisions and in this way were rapidly running in debt, which the company expected us to discharge to them in beaver fur. Their object was to make the most out of us without regard to their previous professions and promises. Finding myself, like most of my comrades, destitute of all means of support and sustenance, of defense and offense, I looked around for something by which I could live in that wild region. On Arriving at the Gros-Ventre village we had found a hunter and trapper named Colter, who had been one of Lewis & Clarke's men, and had returned thus far with them in 1807. Of him I purchased a set of beaver traps for $120, a pound and a half of powder for $6, and a gun for $40. Seeing me thus equipped, Liza, the most active, the meanest and most rascally of the whole, offered me new and good traps, a gun and amunition. I told him he appeared willing enough to help when help was not needed, and after I was provided at my own expense. I then selected two companions, Miller and McDaniel, who had been imposed on by the bourgeoise in the same manner with myself, and in their company I prepared to begin business. These two had, by good fortune bought with them six traps, two guns and amunition of their own. We cut down a tree and of the trunk made a canoe in which we prepared to ascend to the "Forks" and head waters of the Missouri and the mountains. We were young, and sanguine of success. No fears of the future clouded our

prospects and the adventures that lay before us excited
our hopes and fancies to the highest pitch. "No dangers
daunted and no labors tired us." Before leaving the Fort
and my old companions, I will relate a characteristic anec-
dote of Cheek, who so soon after this, expiated his fol-
lies by a violent death. In an early part of the voyage,
when coming up the river, about two months before, I
had sent Cheek to draw our share of provisions from the
provision boat. Francois Ried, who dealt them out for the
company, offered Cheek a bear's head, saying it was good
enough for "you fellows," by this meaning the Americans.
Cheek returned to his boat in great rage at the insult, as
he deemed it, and threatened to whip him (Ried) for the
said contumely on himself and fellow companions, as soon
as he was out of Government employ—that is, as soon as
we had delivered up Shehaka to the Mandans. The matter
passed on and I supposed was forgotten by Cheek himself, until the Fort was built, and the Americans were
about separating with many grievances unredressed and
wrongs unavenged. Cheek meeting Ried one morning on
the bank of the river, told him that he had promised to
whip him and that he could not break his word on any
account. He thereupon struck at the audacious Frenchman, who had presumed to call Americans "fellows," and
offer them a bear's head. Ried saved himself by running
aboard one of the boats, where he obtained a reinforcement. Cheek beat a retreat, and a truce was observed by
both parties till night fall. I had encamped with Cheek
and two others, a few hundred yards above the Fort. We
were all, except Cheek, in the tent, about nine o'clock in
the evening, when Ried with a company, all armed with
pistols and dirks came up and demanded to see Cheek,
saying that he had attacked him within the lines of the
Fort, when he knew he could not fight without violating
orders. I told him that Cheek was not in the tent. "He is

hid, the cowardly rascal," cried Ried, and went to search-
ing the bushes. After he and his company were gone, I
found Cheek at Major Henry's tent, amusing himself with
cards and wine. I took him with me to our own tent, fearing that Ried's company might kill him if they found him
that night. He was silent while hearing my account and
for some minutes after entering our tent. He then spoke
as if on maturest reflection, and said that he had intended
to have let Ried go, with what he had got, "but now I
will whip him in the morning if I lose my life by it." In
the morning he started unarmed and wrapped in his
blanket for the Fort. I with a few others followed to see
fair play which is ever a jewel with the American. Cheek
soon found Ried and accosted him in front of the Fort, by
informing him that he had came down to accommodate
him with the interview which he had understood had
been sought for, so anxiously the night before. Ried said
he was in liquor the night before—wanted to have nothing to do with him and began to make for the Fort. "You
must catch a little anyhow" said Cheek, and springing
towards Ried like a wild cat, with one blow he felled him
to the earth. Capt. Chouteau who had seen the whole proceeding from the Fort, immediately rushed out with
about thirty of his men all armed. "Bring out the irons,
seize him, seize him," cried Chouteau, frantic with passion,
and raging like a mad bull. Cheek prudently retired to
our company on the bank of the river, a short distance,
and said he would die rather than be ironed. We were
ready to stand by him to the last. Chouteau now ordered
his men to fire on us and the next moment would have
seen blood-shed and the death of some of us, had not
L'Abbadieu, Valle, Menard, Morrison, Henry and one of
Chouteau's sons thrown themselves between us and the
opposite party and thus preventing the execution of
Chouteau's order. Him they forced back, struggling like

a mad child in its mothers arms into the Fort. On the next day after this fracas, Miller, McDaniel and myself parted from our companions after agreeing to meet them again on the Forks or head-waters of the Missouri and started in our canoe up the river. The river is very crooked in this part and much narrower than we had found it below. We came to a Mandan village on the south side of the stream on the day of our departure from the Fort. On arriving here, we were on the north side of the river, and on account of the violence of the wind, did not cross to the village. Late in the evening a woman in attempting to cross in a skin canoe, was overset in the middle of the river. She was seen from the village, and immediately, a multitude of men rushed into the water and seemed to run rather than swim to the woman whom they rescued from the water with wonderful rapidity. Their dexterity in swimming was truly astonishing to us. We pushed or rather paddled on in a shower of rain, till late that night and encamped. In the morning we went on in a snowstorm and in four days the ice floating in the river, prevented further navigation of the stream with the canoe. We stopped on the south side of the river, built a small cabin, banked it round with earth and soon made ourselves quite comfortable. This was in the month of November. We had caught a few beaver skins in our route from the Gros-Ventre village, and were employed ourselves in making moccasins and leggins and in killing game which was very plenty all around us. Here we determined to pass the winter and in the Spring continue our ascent of the Missouri to the Forks. On Chistmas day I froze my feet and became so disabled as to be confined to the house unable to walk. Miller and McDaniel soon after started back for the Fort, with our stock of beaver skins to exchange them for ammunition. They were gone twice the length of time agreed on for their stay. I began

to consume the last of my rations and should have suffered for food, had not a company of friendly Indians
called at the cabin and bartered provisions for trinkets
and tobacco. My next visitors were two Canadians and an
American named Ayers, from the Fort, who were going
on with despatches for the main company, that was supposed to be at Manual's Fort at the mouth of the Big
Horn, a branch of the Yellow Stone. These men informed
me that Miller and McDaniel had changed their mind;
that they did not intend to continue further up the river
and seemed to be in no haste to return to me. They urged
me to accompany them, and promised me the use of one
of their horses till my feet should become well enough
for me to walk. I consented to go with them and prepared
to leave my cabin. Before doing so, I buried the traps and
other accoutrements of my two former companions in a
corner of the lodge, and pealing off the bark from a log
above them, I wrote on it, "In this corner your things
lie" I learned on my return in the Spring that both of
them had been killed as was supposed by the Rickarees.
Their guns, traps, &c., were seen in the hands of some
of that tribe; but they were never heard of afterwards.

On the third of February, 1810, eight months after my
departure from St. Louis, I started from my winter lodge;
but I soon repented my undertaking. The horses were all
too weak to carry more than the load appropriated to
them, and I was thus compelled to walk. My feet became
very sore and gave me great pain, while the crust on the
snow made the traveling of all of us, both slow and difficult. I suffered severely at starting but gradually improved
in strength and was able in a few days to keep up with
less torture to myself than at first. We ascended the south
bank of the river till we struck the Little Missouri a
branch from the south. Here we found some Indians who
advised us to keep up the banks of this river for two days,

and then turning northwardly, a half-days travel would bring us to the Gunpowder river near its head: this is a branch of the Yellow Stone. We travelled two days as directed and left the Little Missouri in search of the river. We missed it entirely, on account of our traveling so much slower than the Indians are accustomed to do. Over two day's travel was not greater than one of theirs. For five days we kept our course to the north in an open plain, and in the heart of winter. The cold was intense and the wind from the mountains most piercing. The snow blew directly in our faces and ice was formed on our lips and eyebrows. In this high latitude and in the open prairies in the vicinity of the mountains where we then were, the winters are very cold. On the first night we were covered where we lay to the depth of three feet by the snow. No game was to be seen and we were destitute of provisions. For five days we tasted not a morsel of food, and not even the means of making a fire. We saw not a mound or hill, tree or shrub, not a beast nor a bird until the fifth day when we discried afar off a high mound. We were destitute, alone in that vast desolate and to us limitless expanse, of drifting snow, which the winds drove into our faces and heaped around our steps. Snow was our only food and drink, and snow made our covering at night. We suffered dreadfully from hunger. On the first and second days after leaving the Little Missouri for the desert we were now traversing, our appetites were sharper and the pangs of hunger more intense than afterwards. A languor and faintness succeeded which made travelling most laborious and painful. On the fifth day we had lost so much of strength and felt such weakness for want of food, that the most terrible of deaths, a death by famine, stared us in the face. The pangs and miseries we endured are vividly described by Mr. Kendall, from actual experience in his "Santa Fe Expedition."

My feet, in addition to all other sufferings, now became sore and more painful than ever. The men had made for me a moccasin of skin taken from the legs of a buffalo, and which I wore with the hair next my feet and legs. I felt the blood gurgling and bubbling in this casing at every step. We were about to ward off starvation by killing a horse, and eating the raw flesh and blood, when on the fifth day of our wandering in this wilderness a mound was seen, as above mentioned, in the distance. We reached and ascended it in the evening, whence we saw woods and buffaloes before us. We hastened to kill several of these noblest of all animals of game, and encamped in the woods, where we quickly made a fire and cut up the meat. We were all so voracious in our appetites, as not to wait for the cooking, but ate great quantities nearly raw. The first taste, stimulated our languor and appetites to an ungovernable pitch. We ate and ate and ate, as if there were no limit to our capacity, and no quantity could satisfy us. At length when gorged to the full and utterly unable to hold any more, we gave out and sought repose about midnight under our tents. But sleep fled from our eyes and in the morning we arose, without having rested, feverish and more fatigued than when we supped and retired the night before. Our feet, limbs and bodies were swollen and bloated, and we all found ourselves laid up on the sick list, by our debauch on buffaloe meat. We had no desire to eat again on that day, and remained in camp utterly unable to travel, till the next morning, when we started forward, travelling slowly. We soon struck the river which we had suffered so much in seeking, and bent our course up the stream, crossing its bends on the ice. On one occasion when saving distance by cutting off a bend of the river, the horse carrying my pack and worldly goods, fell into an air hole and would have instantly disappeared had I not caught him by the tail and dragged

him out to some distance, with a risk to myself of plunging under the ice into a rapid current, that made me
shudder the moment I coolly looked at the danger. Hair
breadth escapes from death are so frequent in the life of a
hunter in this wild region as to lose all novelty and may
seem unworthy of mention. I shall relate a few as I proceed, for the purpose of shewing the slight tenure the
pioneer holds of life. And yet Boone, the prince of the
prairies, "lived hunting up to ninety." Perhaps pure air
and continual exercise are more than a counterbalance
toward a long life, against all the dangers of a hunters and
trappers existence, even among hostile savages, such as
we were now rapidly approaching.

We continued our course up the Yellow Stone, gradually recovering from the effects of our unnatural surfeit
and gross gormandizing of buffalo meat. The country here
is one immense, level plain, and abounded, at this time,
with large herds of buffalo, which subsisted on the buds
of trees and the grass which the powerful winds laid bare
of snow in many places. The river was skirted on either
side by woods. At last, after fifteen days of painful travel
and much suffering, we reached "Manuel's Fort," at the
mouth of the Big Horn, where I found the most of my
crew, and a small detachment of the company's men from
whom I had parted the previous fall. This Fort, as before
mentioned, was built by Liza in the spring of 1808, and
a small garrison left in it, who had remained there ever
since. Here I found Cheek, Brown, Dougherty and the
rest of my crew rejoicing to see me. I was not a little surprised to find Col. Pierre Menard in command, who was
to have returned to St. Louis from the Fort at the Gros
Ventre village, and Liza intended to take command of
the party on the head waters of the Missouri. Such was
the arrangement at the commencement of the voyage. I
soon learned from the men what they supposed to be the

cause of the change. The next day after I had left the Fort on the Missouri, in the fall, Cheek and several Americans were in the office or *marque* of the company, endeavoring to get their equipments according to contract. Liza was present. Chouteau's name was mentioned in the course of the conversation, when Cheek cooly remarked that if he caught Chouteau a hundred yards from camp he would shoot him. "Cheek! Cheek!!" exclaimed Liza, "mind what you say." "I do that," said Cheek, "and Liza, I have heard some of our boys say that if they ever caught you two hundred yards from camp they would shoot you, and if they don't I will. You ought not to expect any thing better from the Americans after having treated them with so much meanness, treachery and cruelty as you have. Now Liza," continued he, "you are going to the forks of the Missouri, mark my words, you will never come back alive." Liza's cheeks blanched at this bold and reckless speech from a man who always performed his promises, whether good or evil. He returned to St. Louis and sent up Col. Menard's in his place. Col. M. was an honorable, high minded gentleman and enjoyed our esteem in a higher degree than any other at the company. Liza we thoroughly detested and despised, both for his acts and his reputation. There were many tales afloat concerning villainies said to have been perpetrated by him on the frontiers. These may have been wholly false or greatly exaggerated, but in his looks there was no deception. Rascality sat on every feature of his dark complexioned, Mexican face—gleamed from his black, Spanish, eyes, and seemed enthroned in a forehead "villainous low." We were glad to be relieved of his presence. After remaining at this Fort or camp a few days we started westward for the "Forks" and mountains in a company of thirty-two men, French and Americans. On first arriving at the Fort I had learned that two of the men

with an Indian chief of the Snake tribe and his two wives
and a son had gone forward, with the intention of killing
game for our company and awaiting our approach on the
route. Our second day's journey brought us to an Indian
lodge; stripped, and near by, we saw a woman and boy
lying on the ground, with their heads split open, evidently by a tomahawk. These were the Snake's elder wife
and son, he having saved himself and his younger wife
by flight on horseback. Our two men who had started out
in company with him, were not molested. They told us
that a party of Gros Ventres had come upon them, committed these murders, and passed on as if engaged in a
lawful and praiseworthy business. These last were the
most powerful and warlike Indians of that region. The
poor Snake tribe, on the contrary, were the weakest, and
consequently became the prey and victims of the others.
They inhabit the caves and chasms of the mountains and
live a miserable and precarious life in eluding the pursuit
of enemies. All the neighboring tribes were at war with
these poor devils. Every party we met pretended to be
out on an expedition against the Snakes, when they frequently reduce to slavery. Thus the strong prey upon the
weak in savage as well as civilized life.

Our course now lay to the north-west for the Forks of
the Missouri, which meet in latitude——among the mountains, whence the last named river runs directly north as
high as latitude——miles, where it turns to the south and
south east, which last course it generally holds to its junction with the Mississippi. On the evening of the day when
we left Manuel's Fort, my friend Brown became blind
from the reflection of the sun on the snow; his eyes pained
him so much that he implored us to put an end to his tor-
ment by shooting him. I watched him during that night
for fear he would commit the act himself. He complained
that his eye balls had bursted, and moaned and groaned

most piteously. In the morning, I opened the swollen lids, and informed him to his great joy that the balls were whole and sound. He could now distinguish a faint glimmering of light. I led him all that day and the next, on the third he had so far recovered that he could see, though but indistinctly. Our guide on this route was Colter, who thoroughly knew the road, having twice escaped over it from capture and death at the hands of the Indians. In ten or twelve days after leaving the Fort we reentered an opening or gap in the mountains, where it commenced snowing most violently and so continued all night. The morning showed us the heads and backs of our horses just visible above the snow which had crushed down all our tents. We proceeded on with the greatest difficulty. As we entered the ravine or opening of the mountain the snow greatly increased in depth being in places from fifty to sixty feet on the ground, a third of which had fallen and drifted in that night. The wind had heaped it up in many places to a prodigious height. The strongest horses took the front to make a road for us, but soon gave out and the ablest bodied men took their places as pioneers. A horse occasionally stepped out of the beaten track and sunk entirely out of sight in the snow. By night we had made about four miles for that day's travel. By that night we passed the ravine and reached the Gallatin river, being the eastern fork of the Missouri. The river sweeps rapidly by the pass at its western extremity, on each side of which the mountain rises perpendicularly from the bank of the river; and apparently stopped our progress up and down the east side of the stream. I forded it and was followed by Dougherty, Ware, and another, when Colter discovered an opening through the mountain on the right or north side, and through it led the rest of the company. We, however, proceeded down the left bank of the river till night, when we en-

camped and supped (four of us) on a piece of buffalo
meat about the size of the two hands. During this and the
proceeding day we suffered from indistinct vision, similar to Brown's affliction of leaving the Big Horn. We all
now became blind as he had been, from the reflection of
the sun's rays on the snow. The hot tears trickled from
the swollen eyes nearly blistering the cheeks, and the
eye-balls seemed bursting from our heads. At first, the
sight was obscured as by a silk veil or handkerchief, and
we were unable to hunt. Now we could not even see our
way before us, and in this dreadful situation we remained
two days and nights. Hunger was again inflicting its sharp
pangs upon us, and we were upon the point of killing one
of the pack horses, when on the fourth day after crossing
the Gallatin, one of the men killed a goose, of which,
being now somewhat recovered from our blindness, we
made a soup and stayed the gnawings of hunger. The
next day our eyes were much better, and we fortunately
killed an elk, of which we ate without excess, being
taught by experience, the dangers of gluttony after a fast.
We continued on down the river and soon came in sight
of our comrades in the main body on the right bank.
They, like ourselves, had all been blind, and had suffered more severely than we from the same causes. They
had killed three dogs, one a present to me from an Indian, and two horses to appease the demands of hunger
before they had sufficiently recovered to take sight on
their guns. Which in this distressed situation enveloped
by thick darkness at midday, thirty Snake Indians came
among them, and left without committing any depredation. Brown and another, who suffered less than the
others, saw and counted these Indians, who might have
killed them all and escaped with their effects with perfect
impunity. Their preservation was wonderful. When we
overtook them they were slowly recovering from blind-

ness and we all encamped together, with thankful and joyous hearts for our late narrow escape from painful and lingering death. We proceeded on in better spirits. On the next day we passed a battle field of the Indians, where the skulls and bones were lying around on the ground in vast numbers. The battle which had caused this terrible slaughter, took place in 1808, the year but one before, between the Black-Feet to the number of fifteen hundred on the one side, and the Flat-Heads and Crows, numbering together about eight hundred on the other. Colter was in the battle on the side of the latter, and was wounded in the leg, and thus disabled from standing. He crawled to a small thicket and there loaded and fired while sitting on the ground. The battle was desperately fought on both sides, but victory remained with the weaker party. The Black-Feet engaged at first with about five hundred Flat-Heads, whom they attacked in great fury. The noise, shouts and firing brought a reinforcement of Crows to the Flat-Heads, who were fighting with great spirit and defending the ground manfully. The Black-Feet who are the Arabs of this region, were at length repulsed, but retired in perfect order and could hardly be said to have been defeated. The Flat-Heads are a noble race of men, brave, generous and hospitable. They might be called the Spartans of Oregon. Lewis & Clark had received much kindness from them in their expedition to the Columbia, which waters their country; and at the time of this well fought battle, Colter was leading them to Manuel's Fort to trade with the Americans, when the Black Feet fell upon them in such numbers as seemingly to make their destruction certain. Their desperate courage saved them from a general massacre.

The following day we reached the long sought "Forks of the Missouri," or the place of confluence of the Gallatin, Madison and Jefferson rivers. Here at last, after ten months of travel, we encamped, commenced a Fort in the point made by the Madison and Jefferson forks, and prepared to begin business. This point was the scene of Colter's escape in the fall of the year but one before, from the Indians and a death by torture; an event so extraordinary and thrilling, as he related it to me, that it deserves a brief narration.

NOTE.—The following is the description given by G. W. KENDALL, of the sufferings from starvation, referred to on the 19th page.

"For the first two days through which a strong and hearty man is doomed to exist upon nothing, his sufferings are, perhaps, more acute than in the remaining stages. He feels an inordinate, unappeasable, craving at the stomach, night and day. The mind runs upon beef, bread and other substantials; but still in a great measure, the body retains its strength. On the third and fourth days, but especially on the fourth, this incessant craving gives place to a sinking and weakness of the stomach, accompanied by nausea. The unfortunate sufferer still desires food, but with loss of strength he loses that eager craving which is felt in the earlier stages. Should he chance to obtain a morsel or two of food, as was occasionally the case with us, he swallows it with a wolfish avidity; but five minutes afterwards his sufferings are more intense than ever. He feels as if he had swallowed a living lobster, which is clawing and feeding upon the very foundations of his existence. On the fifth day his cheeks suddenly appear hollow and sunken, his body attenuated, his color an ashy pale, and his eye wild, glassy, cannibalish. The different parts of the system now wage war with each other. The stomach calls upon the legs to go with it, in quest of food: the legs from very weakness refuse. The sixth day brings with it incessant suffering, although the pangs of hunger are lost in an overpowering langor and sickness. The head becomes giddy—the ghosts of well remembered dinners pass in hideous procession through the mind. The seventh day comes bringing in train lassitude and further prostration of the system. The arms hang listlessly, the legs drag heavily. The desire for food is stll left, to a degree, but it must be brought, not sought. The miserable remnant of life which still hangs to the sufferer is a burden almost too grievous to be borne; yet his inherent love of existence induces a desire still to preserve it, if it can be saved without a tax upon bodily exertion. The mind wanders. At one moment he thinks his weary limbs cannot sustain him a mile—the next he is endowed with unnatural strength, and if there be a certainty of relief before him, dashes bravely and strongly onward, wondering where proceeds this new and sudden impulse. Farther than this my experience runneth not."—Vol. I. p. 266. The whole of the company—ninety eight men—subsisted for thirteen days on what was "really not provisions enough for three, and then came upon a herd of 17000 sheep, about eighty miles south east of Santa fe. Here a scene of feasting ensued which beggars description.   *   *   *   Our men abandoned themselves at once to eating—perhaps I should rather call it gormandizing or stuffing.   *   *   *   Had the food been any thing but mutton, and had we not procured an ample supply of salt from the Mexicans to season it, our men might have died of the surfeit."—p. 265.

This lively writer, Geo. W. Kendall, has told a tale in the book just quoted, of prairie life and adventures as well as of Mexican barbarity and treachery, and his embellished his story with all the graces of style and description calculated to render it a work of enduring interest.

CHAPTER II

Colter's Race and escapes—Separation for trapping—Descent of
the Missouri—A fine Landscape—Bad luck—Alarm from Indians—Retreat to the Fort—Death of Cheek—Pursuit of the
Indians—Return—The White Bears—Incidents of hunting—Return to the Twenty Five Yard river—A party of Gros Ventres—
Suspected Robbery—Interview with the Crows—Rapid crossing
of the Yellow Stone—Descent to the Fort and the *"Cache"*—
Robbery made certain—Passage to the Missouri—Indian character and customs—A Spree, ending almost tragically—Generosity
of the Company—Settlement with them—A sage reflection.

WHEN COLTER was returning in 1807 with Lewis & Clark,
from Oregon, he met a company of hunters ascending the
Missouri, by whom he was persuaded to return to the
trapping region, to hunt and trap with them. Here he was
found by Liza in the following year, whom he assisted in
building the Fort at the Big Horn. In one of his many
excursions from this post to the Forks of the Missouri, for
beaver, he made the wonderful escape adverted to in the
last chapter and which I give precisely as he related it to
me. His veracity was never questioned among us and his
character was that of a true American backwoodsman. He
was about thirty-five years of age, five feet ten inches in
height and wore an open, ingenious, and pleasing countenance of the Daniel Boone stamp. Nature had formed
him, like Boone, for hardy endurance of fatigue, priva-
tions and perils. He had gone with a companion named
Potts to the Jefferson river, which is the most western of
the three Forks, and runs near the base of the mountains.

29

They were both proceeding up the river in search of beaver, each in his own canoe, when a war party of about eight hundred Black-Feet Indians suddenly appeared on the east bank of the river. The Chiefs ordered them to come ashore, and apprehending robbery only, and knowing the utter hopelessness of flight and having dropped his traps over the side of the canoe from the Indians, into the water, which was here quite shallow, he hastened to obey their mandate. On reaching the shore, he was seized, disarmed and stripped entirely naked. Potts was still in his canoe in the middle of the stream, where he remained stationary, watching the result. Colter requested him to come ashore, which he refused to do, saying he might as well lose his life at once, as be stripped and robbed in the manner Colter had been. An Indian immediately fired and shot him about the hip; he dropped down in the canoe, but instantly rose with his rifle in his hands. "Are you hurt," said Colter. "Yes, said he, too much hurt to escape; if you can get away do so. I will kill at least one of them." He leveled his rifle and shot an Indian dead. In an instant, at least a hundred bullets pierced his body and as many savages rushed into the stream and pulled the canoe, containing his riddled corpse, ashore. They dragged the body up onto the bank, and with their hatchets and knives cut and hacked it all to pieces, and limb from limb. The entrails, heart, lungs, &c., they threw into Colter's face. The relations of the killed Indian were furious with rage and struggled, with tomahawk in hand, to reach Colter, while others held them back. He was every moment expecting the death blow or the fatal shot that should lay him beside his companion. A council was hastily held over him and his fate quickly determined upon. He expected to die by tomahawk, slow, lingering and horrible. But they had magnanimously determined to give him a chance, though a slight one, for his life. After the council, a Chief pointed to the prairie and motioned him away with his hand, saying in the Crow language, "go—go away." He supposed they intended to shoot him as soon as he was out of the crowd and presented a fair mark to their guns. He started in a walk, and an old Indian with impatient signs and exclamations, told him to go faster, and as he still kept a walk, the same Indian manifested his wishes by still more violent gestures and adjurations. When he had gone a distance of eighty or a hundred yards from the army of his enemies, he saw the younger Indians throwing off their blankets, leggings, and other incumbrances, as if for a race. Now he knew their object. He was to run a race, of which the prize was to be his own life and scalp. Off he started with the speed of the wind. The war-whoop and yell immediately arose behind him; and looking back, he saw a large company of young warriors, with spears, in rapid pursuit. He ran with all the strength that nature, excited to the utmost, could give; fear and hope lent a supernatural vigor to his limbs and the rapidity of his flight astonished himself. The Madison Fork lay directly before him, five miles from his starting place. He had run half the distance when his strength began to fail and the blood to gush from his nostrils. At every leap the red stream spurted before him, and his limbs were growing rapidly weaker and weaker. He stopped and looked back; he had far outstripped all his pursuers and could get off if strength would only hold out. One solitary Indian, far ahead of the others, was rapidly approaching, with a spear in his right hand, and a blanket streaming behind from his left hand and shoulder. Despairing of escape, Colter awaited his pursuer and called to him in the Crow language, to save his life. The savage did not seem to hear him, but letting go his blanket, and seizing his spear with both hands, he rushed at Colter, naked and defenseless as he stood before him and made a desperate lunge to transfix him. Colter seized the spear, near the head, with his right hand, and exerting his whole strength, aided by the weight of the falling Indian, who had lost his balance in the fury of the onset, he broke off the iron head or blade which remained in his hand, while the savage fell to the ground and lay prostrate and disarmed before him. Now was *his* turn to beg for his life, which he did in the Crow language, and held up his hands imploringly, but Colter was not in a mood to remember the golden rule, and pinned his adversary through the body to the earth one stab with the spear head. He quickly drew the weapon from the body of the now dying Indian, and seizing his blanket as lawful spoil, he again set out with renewed strength, feeling, he said to me, as if he had not run a mile. A shout and yell arose from the pursuing army in his rear as from a legion of devils, and he saw the prairie behind him covered with Indians in full and rapid chase. Before him, if any where was life and safety; behind him certain death; and running as never man before sped the foot, except, perhaps, at the Olympic Games, he reached his goal, the Madison river and the end of his five mile heat. Dashing through the willows on the bank he plunged into the stream and saw close beside him a beaver house, standing like a coal-pit about ten feet above the surface of the water, which was here of about the same depth. This presented to him a refuge from his ferocious enemies of which he immediately availed himself. Diving under the water he arose into the beaver house, where he found a dry and comfortable resting place on the upper floor or story of this singular structure. The Indians soon came up, and in their search for him they stood upon the roof of his house of refuge, which he expected every moment to hear them breaking open. He also feared that they would set it on fire. After a diligent search on that side of the

river, they crossed over, and in about two hours returned
again to his temporary habitation in which he was enjoying bodily rest, though with much anxious foreboding.
The beaver houses are divided into two stories and will
generally accommodate several men in a dry and comfortable lodging. In this asylum Colter kept fast till night.
The cries of his terrible enemies had gradually died away,
and all was still around him, when he ventured out of his
hiding place, by the same opening under the water by
which he entered and which admits the beavers to their
building. He swam the river and hastened towards the
mountain gap or ravine, about thirty miles above on the
river, through which our company passed in the snow
with so much difficulty. Fearing that the Indians might
have guarded this pass, which was the only outlet from
the valley, and to avoid the danger of a surprise, Colter
ascended the almost perpendicular mountain before him,
the tops and sides of which a great way down, were covered with perpetual snow. He clambered up this fearful
ascent about four miles below the gap, holding on by the
rocks, shrubs and branches of trees, and by morning had
reached the top. He lay there concealed all that day, and
at night proceeded on in the descent of the mountain,
which he accomplished by dawn. He now hastened on in
the open plain towards Manuel's Fort on the Big Horn,
about three hundred miles a headin the north-east. He
travelled day and night, stopping only for necessary repose, and eating roots and the bark of trees for eleven
days. He reached the Fort, nearly exhausted by hunger,
fatigue and excitement. His only clothing was the Indian's
blanket, whom he had killed in the race, and his only
weapon, the same Indian's spear which he brought to the
Fort as a trophy. His beard was long, his face and whole
body were thin and emaciated by hunger, and his limbs
and feet swollen and sore. The company at the Fort did

not recognize him in this dismal plight until he had made himself known. Colter now with me passed over the scene of his capture and wonderful escape, and described his emotions during the whole adventure with great minuteness. Not the least of his exploits was the scaling of the mountain, which seemed to me impossible even by the mountain goat. As I looked at its rugged and perpendicular sides I wondered how he ever reached the top—a feat probably never performed before by mortal man. The whole affair is a fine example of the quick and ready thoughtfulness and presence of mind in a desperate situation, and the power of endurance, which characterise the western pioneer. As we passed over the ground where Colter ran his race, and listened to his story an undefinable fear crept over all. We felt awe-struck by the nameless and numerous dangers that evidently beset us on every side. Even Cheek's courage sunk and his hitherto buoyant and cheerful spirit was depressed at hearing of the perils of the place. He spoke despondingly and his mind was uneasy, restless and fearful. "I am afraid," said he, "and I acknowledge it. I never felt fear before but now I feel it." A melancholy that seemed like a presentiment of his own fate, possessed him, and to us he was serious almost to sadness, until he met his death a few days afterwards from the same Blackfeet from whom Colter escaped. Colter told us the particulars of a second adventure which I will give to the reader. In the winter when he had recovered from the fatigues of his long race and journey, he wished to recover the traps which he had dropped into the Jefferson Fork on the first appearance of the Indians who captured him. He supposed the Indians were all quiet in winter quarters, and retraced his steps to the Gallatin Fork. He had just passed the mountain gap, and encamped on the bank of the river for the night and kindled a fire to cook his supper of buffalo meat

when he heard the crackling of leaves and branches behind him in the direction of the river. He could see nothing, it being quite dark, but quickly he heard the cocking
of guns and instantly leaped over the fire. Several shots
followed and bullets whistled around him, knocking the
coals off his fire over the ground. Again he fled for life,
and the second time, ascended the perpendicular mountain which he had gone up in his former flight fearing
now as then, that the pass might be guarded by Indians.
He reached the top before morning and resting for the
day descended the next night, and then made his way
with all possible speed, to the Fort. He said that at the
time, he promised God Almighty that he would never
return to this region again if he were only permitted to
escape once more with his life. He did escape once more,
and was now again in the same country, courting the
same dangers, which he had so often braved, and that
seemed to have for him a kind of fascination. Such men,
and there are thousands of such, can only live in a state
of excitement and constant action. Perils and danger are
their natural element and their familiarity with them and
indifference to their fate, are well illustrated in these adventures of Colter.

A few days afterward, when Cheek was killed and Colter had another narrow escape, he came into the Fort,
and said he had promised his Maker to leave the country,
and "now" said he, throwing down his hat on the ground,
"If God will only forgive me this time and let me off I
will leave the country day after tomorrow—and be d—d
if I ever come into it again." He left accordingly, in company with young Bryant of Philadelphia, whose father
was a merchant of that city, and one other whose name
I forget. They were attacked by the Blackfeet just beyond
the mountains, but escaped by hiding in a thicket, where
the Indians were afraid to follow them, and at night they

proceeded towards the Big Horn, lying concealed in the daytime. They reached St. Louis safely and a few years after I heard of Colter's death by jaundice.

We arrived at the Forks of the Missouri on the third day of April, 1810, ten months after leaving St. Louis and two months and one day after quitting my cabin above the Gros Ventre village. We had now reached our place of business, trapping for beaver, and prepared to set to work. Dougherty, Brown, Ware and myself agreed to trap in company on the Missouri between the Forks and the Falls, which lie several hundred miles down the river to the north, from the Forks. We made two canoes by hollowing out the trunks of two trees and on the third or fourth day after our arrival at the Forks we were ready to start on an expedition down the river. The rest of the Americans with a few French, in all eighteen in number, determined to go up the Jefferson river for trapping, and the rest of the company under Col. Menard remained to complete the Fort and trading house at the Forks between the Jefferson and Madison rivers. On parting from Cheek, he said in a melancholy tone, "James you are going down the Missouri, and it is the general opinion that you will be killed. The Blackfeet are at the falls, encamped I hear, and we fear you will never come back. But I am afraid for myself as well as you. I know not the cause, but I have felt fear ever since I came to the Forks, and I never was afraid of anything before. You may come out safe, and I may be killed. Then you will say, there was Cheek afraid to go with us down the river for fear of death, and now he has found his grave by going up the river. I may be dead when you return." His words made little impression on me at the time, but his tragical end a few days afterwards recalled them to my mind and stamped them on my memory forever. I endeavored to persuade him to join our party, while he was equally urgent for me to join his, saying that if we went in one company our force would afford more protection from Indians, than in small parties, while I contended that the fewer our numbers the better would be our chance of concealment and escape from any war parties that might be traversing the country. We parted never to meet again, taking opposite directions and both of us going into the midst of dangers. My company of four started down the river and caught some beaver on the first day. On the second we passed a very high spur of the mountain on our right. The mountains in sight on our left, were not so high as those to the east of us. On the third day we issued from very high and desolate mountains on both sides of us, whose tops are covered with snow throughout the year, and came upon a scene of beauty and magnificence combined, unequalled by any other view of nature that I ever beheld. It really realized all my conception of the Garden of Eden. In the west the peaks and pinnacles of the Rocky Mountains shone resplendent in the sun. The snow on their tops sent back a beautiful reflection of the rays of the morning sun. From the sides of the dividing ridge between the waters of the Missouri and Columbia, there sloped gradually down to the bank of the river we were on, a plain, then covered with every variety of wild animals peculiar to this region, while on the east another plain arose by a very gradual ascent, and extended as far as the eye could reach. These and the mountain sides were dark with Buffalo, Elk, Deer, Moose, wild Goats and wild Sheep; some grazing, some lying down under the trees and all enjoying a perfect millenium of peace and quiet. On the margin the swan, geese, and pelicans, cropped the grass or floated on the surface of the water. The cotton wood trees seemed to have been planted by the hand of man on the bank of the river to shade our way, and the pines and cedars waved their tall, majestic heads along the base and on the sides of the mountains. The whole landscape was that of the most splendid English park. The stillness, beauty and loveliness of this scene, stuck us all with indescribable emotions. We rested on the oars and enjoyed the whole view in silent astonishment and admiration. Nature seemed to have rested here, after creating the wild mountains and chasms among which we had voyaged for two days. Dougherty, as if inspired by the scene with the spirit of poetry and song, broke forth in one of Burns' noblest lyrics, which found a deep echo in our hearts. We floated on till evening through this most delightful country, when we stopped and prepared supper on the bank of the river. We set our traps and before going to rest for the night we examined them and found a beaver in every one, being twenty-three in all. In the evening we were nearly as successful as before and were cheered with thoughts of making a speedy fortune. We determined to remain in this second paradise as long as our pursuits would permit. We skinned our beaver, ate breakfast and started to go further down the river in search of a good camp ground. Brown and Dougherty started in a canoe, before Ware and I were ready, and after going about two hundred yards, they struck a rock concealed under the water, overturned the canoe, and lost all our skins and amunition except the little powder in our horns and few skins left behind. They also lost their guns, but saved themselves and the canoe. Ware and I soon followed them, and we all encamped at the mouth of a small creek on the left side of the river. Here Ware and I remained while the two others went back to the Fort to procure other guns and amunition, taking with them one of our guns. They reached the Fort the first night, having saved a great distance by crossing the country and cutting off the bend of the river which here makes a large sweep to the east. They went up on the west side or that next to the mountains, waded Jefferson's Fork and entered the Fort late at night. Early the next morning the whole garrison was aroused by an alarm made by Valle and several Frenchmen who came in, as if pursued by enemies, and informed them that the whole party who had gone up the Jefferson, at the time of our departure down the Missouri, had been killed by the Indians, and that they expected an immediate attack on the Fort. The whole garrison prepared for resistance. The next morning after Valle's arrival, Colter came in unhurt, with a few others, and said there were no Indians near the Fort. Col. Menard despatched Dougherty and Brown, on the same day, to us with the request that we should hasten to the Fort to assist in its defense. Being well mounted, they came up to our camp as we were preparing dinner. Their faces were pale with fright, and in great trepidation they told us they had seen Indian *"signs"* on the route from the Fort—that a horse with a rope about his neck had run up and snuffed around them as if in search of his master, and then disappeared—that an Indian dog had performed the same action. Every thing indicated that Indians were near, and we hastened to depart for the Fort. We proceeded up the creek near whose mouth we had encamped, and were screened from view on the north by the willows on our right. We had gone very cautiously four miles, when we left the river, and I perceived a small herd of buffalo in the creek bottom far to our right, start bounding off as if from pursuers in the rear, and immediately after, I descried through an opening in the willows, eight Indians, walking rapidly across the plain in the direction of our late camp. I informed the others of my observation, and Ware horror stricken proposed immediate flight. I protested against this course and no one seconded him, but we were all alarmed and the chins and lips of some quivered as they spoke. I said that we could not all escape, having but two horses among us, that we had, perhaps, seen the whole force of the Indians, and that they might not have seen us at all; that we could fight eight with success. I proposed that if attacked we should make a breast-work of our horses and two of us should fire upon them at a hundred yards, that the other two should fire at fifty yards, that the reloaded guns should desptach the third couple, and our knives and pistols finish the seventh and eighth. This Bobadil proposition revived their spirits wonderfully, and they instantly dismissed all thoughts of flight. Ware and I ascended a small height to watch the Indians, while the rest went on with the horses, which travelled slowly with packs. Here we saw the Indians go up to our deserted camp, the smoke from which had attracted them thither. The smoke in this clear atmosphere is visible to a great distance. The hunters said they had seen the smoke from an ordinary fire in the prairies for three hundred miles. We proceeded without pursuit, and at two o'clock the next morning we reached the Jefferson Fork, opposite the Fort. Unwilling to risk the danger of an attack by delay we forded the river with great difficulty, and went towards the Fort, whence some dogs rushed upon us, barking furiously. I spoke to the dogs, and a voice hailed us from the Fort with "who's there"? I answered promptly, and thus saved ourselves from a volley, for when we entered the Fort, the whole garrison was drawn up with fingers upon triggers. They were expecting an attack every moment, and did not look for us so soon. They were all in the greatest consternation. Lieutenant Emmel with those before mentioned of the trapping party up the river, had come in and they supposed that all the rest had been killed. They had had a very narrow escape themselves, as all but Colter probably considered it; he with his large experience, naturally looked upon the whole as an ordinary occurrence. During the day others came in and we learned from them the extent of our losses. The company consisting of eighteen, had proceeded up the bank of the Jefferson, trapping, and on the third day had pitched their tents for the night, near the river, and about forty miles from the Fort. Cheek, Hull and Ayers were employed in preparing the camp, while the rest had dispersed in various directions to kill game, when some thirty or forty Indians appeared on the prairie south of them, running a foot and on horses, toward the camp. Valle and two men whose names I forget, came running up to Cheek and others and told them to catch their horses and escape. This Cheek refused to do, but, seizing his rifle and pistols, said he would stay and abide his fate. "My time has come, but I will kill at least two of them, and then I don't care." His gloomy forebodings were about to be fulfilled through his own recklessness and obstinacy. Ayers ran frantically about, paralysed by fear and crying, "O God, O God, what can I do." Though a horse was within his reach he was disabled by terror from mounting and saving his life. Courage and cowardice met the same fate, though in very different manners. Hull stood coolly examining his rifle as if for battle. The enemy were coming swiftly toward them, and Valle and his two companions started off pursued by mounted Indians. The sharp reports of Cheek's rifle and pistols were soon heard, doing the work of death upon the savages, and then a volley of musketry sent the poor fellow to his long home.

Lieutenant Emmel and another came in from hunting, about dusk, ignorant of the fate of their fellows, and seeing the tent gone they supposed the place of the camp had been changed. Hearing a noise at the river, Emmel went down to the bank, whence he saw through the willows, on the opposite side, a camp of thirty Indian lodges, a woman coming down to the river with a brass kettle which he would have sworn was his own, and also a white man bound by both arms to a tree. He could not recognise the prisoner, but supposed he was an American. On returning to the place where Cheek had pitched his tent, he saw his dead body without the scalp, lying where he had bravely met his end. He then hastened to the Fort where his arrival has been noticed before. A greater part of the garrison, with myself, started out on the morning of my coming in to go in pursuit of the Indians, up the river, and to bury our dead. We found and buried the corpses of our murdered comrades, Cheek and Ayers; the latter being found in the river near the bank. Hull was never heard of, and two others, Rucker and Fleehart were also missing; being killed or taken prisoners by the Indians. An Indian was found dead, with two bullets in his body, supposed to be from Cheek's pistol. The body was carefully concealed under leaves and earth, and surrounded by logs. We followed the trail of the savages for two days when we missed it and gave up the chase. Many of the men wished to pursue them into the mountains, but Col. Menard judged it imprudent to go further in search of them, as we should, probably, come upon an army of which this party was but a detachment. He thought the main body was very large, and not distant from us or the Fort, and therefore determined to return and await them there. We accordingly retraced our steps to the Fort, and remained in it, with our whole force, for several days, expecting an attack. No attack was made, however, nor did an enemy make his appearance afterwards, except in the shape of white, grey, brown and grizzly bears. Seeing nothing of our enemies, the Blackfeet, we soon became emboldened and ventured out of the Fort to hunt and trap, to the distance of about six miles. In these short expeditions the men had frequent encounters with bears, which in this region are of enormous size, sometimes weighing 800 pounds each, and when wounded, are the most terribly ferocious and dangerous to the hunter of all other animals. The African Lion and Bengal Tiger are the only beasts of prey, that in ferocity and power, can be compared with the Grey or Grizzly Bear of the Rocky Mountains. These were the terrors of our men as much as were the Indians, and they usually spoke of them both as equally terrible and equally to be avoided. The great strength of the Bear, his swiftness and utter insensibility to danger when wounded, render him as dangerous to the hunter as the Tiger or the Lion. The first shot is seldom fatal upon him, on account of the thickness of his skin and skull, and the great quantity of fat and flesh that envelope his heart, and make an almost impenetrable shield in front. I will relate a few adventures with this North American king of beasts, and then proceed with my narrative.

Ware, an American, was hunting on an island in the Madison river, a short distance from the Fort and came suddenly, in a buffalo path, upon a white or grey Bear. He fired at the monster, wounded him in the breast, and then ran for his life, with the Bear at his heels, and saved himself by plunging into the river. His pursuer laid himself down on the bank and in the last struggle of death, fell into the water, where he died. Ware drew him out, took off the skin and was cutting and hanging up the meat, when he heard the noise of another Bear in the thicket near by. He hastened to the Fort for assistance and a party, with me, went over to the island. When there, we separated in our search, and in beating about the bushes, I, with my dog, entered a narrow path, and had gone some distance, when I saw the dog ahead, suddenly bristle up, bark and walk lightly as if scenting danger. I called to the men to come up, and watched the dog. He soon found the bear guarding a dead elk, which he and his dead companion had killed and covered with

leaves. As soon as he saw the dog he plunged at him, and
came furiously toward me, driving the dog before him
and snorting and raging like a mad bull. I levelled my
gun and snapped, and then ran with the bear at my heels,
and his hot breath upon me. I reached the river bank,
and turned short up a path, in which I met my companions coming to my call. They, however, seeing me
running, were panic stricken and took to their heels also,
thus were we all in full retreat from bruin, who crossed
the river and fled through the willows on the other side.
We heard him crashing his way for many hundred yards.
On another occasion, a party had wounded a bear which
instantly gave chase and overtook a Shawnee Indian in
the company named Luthecaw, who had stumbled over
some brush and fallen. He grasped the Indian by the
double capeau and coat collar and stood over him, while
we fired six shots into the bear, which fell dead upon the
Indian, who cried out that the bear was crushing him to
death, but arose unhurt, as soon as we removed the tremendous weight of the dead monster from his body. His
jaws were firmly closed upon the Shawnee's "capeau" and
coat callar, who arose at last with *"sacre moste, l'est crazy
monte"*—"damn the bear, he almost mashed me."

We kept the flag flying a month, frequently seeing Indians without getting an interview with them; they always fleeing at our approach. We then pulled down the
flag and hoisted the scalp of the Indian whom Cheek had
killed. By this time the Fort was completed and put in
a good state of defense. We subsisted ourselves in the
meantime, by hunting in small parties, which started out
of Fort before day and went some twenty or thirty miles,
and after having killed a buffalo or elk, come back with
the meat loaded on the horses.

The Grizzly Bears frequently made their appearance
and we killed great numbers of them. A Yankee, named

Pelton, was remarkable for his contracted, narrow eyes, which resembled those of a bear. He was a jovial, popular fellow, and had greatly amused the company in coming up the river, by his songs and sermons. At every stopping place he held a meeting for the mock trial of offenders and exhorted us in the New England style to mend our courses and eschew sin. He had an adventure with a bear, about this time, which is worth relating. While trapping near the Fort with a small party, including myself, he was watching his traps alone, a short distance from us, when he heard a rustling in the bushes at his right, and before turning around he was attacked by a large bear, which grasped him by the breast, bore him to the earth and stood over him with his head back and eyes fixed on his face as if observing his features; Pelton screamed and yelled in a most unearthly manner, and his new acquaintance, as if frightened by his appearance and voice, leaped from over his body, stood and looked at him a moment, over his shoulder, growled, and then walked off. We ran in the direction of the cries and soon met Pelton coming towards us in a walk, grumbling and cursing, with his head down, as if he had been disturbed in a comfortable sleep, and altogether wearing an air of great dissatisfaction. He told us the story, and thought he owed his escape to his bearish eyes which disconcerted his friendly relation in the act of making a dinner of him.

The Indians, we thought, kept the game away from the vicinity of the Fort. Thus we passed the time till the month of May, when a party of twenty-one, of whom I was one, determined to go up the Jefferson river to trap. By keeping together we hoped to repel any attack of the savages. We soon found the trapping in such numbers not very profitable, and changed our plan by separating in companies of four, of whom, two men would trap while two watched the camp. In this manner we were engaged, until the fear of Indians began to wear off, and we all became more venturous. One of our company, a Shawnee half-breed named Druyer, the principal hunter of Lewis & Clark's party, went up the river one day and set his traps about a mile from the camp. In the morning he returned alone and brought back six beavers. I warned him of his danger. "I am too much of an Indian to be caught by Indians," said he. On the next day he repeated the adventure and returned with the product of his traps, saying, "this is the way to catch beavers." On the third morning he started again up the river to examine his traps, when we advised him to wait for the whole party, which was about moving further up the stream, and at the same time two other Shawnees left us against our advice, to kill deer. We started forward in company, and soon found the dead bodies of the last mentioned hunters, pierced with lances, arrows and bullets and lying near each other. Further on, about one hundred and fifty yards, Druyer and his horse lay dead, the former mangled in a horrible manner; his head was cut off, his entrails torn out and his body hacked to pieces. We saw from the marks on the ground that he must have fought in a circle on horseback, and probably killed some of his enemies, being a brave man, and well armed with a rifle, pistol, knife and tomahawk. We pursued the trail of the Indians till night, without overtaking them, and then returned, having buried our dead, with saddened hearts to Fort.

Soon after this time, Marie and St. John, my two Canadian companions on the route from my winter quarters on the Missouri to the Big Horn, came to the Fort at the Forks. Marie's right eye was out and he carried the yet fresh marks of a horrible wound on his head and under his jaw. After I had left them at the Big Horn to come to the Forks, they came on to the Twenty-five Yard river, the most western branch of the Yellow Stone, for the purpose of trapping. One morning after setting his traps, Marie strolled out into the prairie for game, and soon perceived a large White Bear rolling on the ground in the shade of a tree. Marie fired at and missed him. The bear snuffed around him without rising, and did not see the hunter until he had re-loaded, fired again and wounded him. His majesty instantly, with ears set back, flew towards his enemy like an arrow, who ran for life, reached a beaver dam across the river, and seeing no escape by land, plunged into the water above the dam. The Bear followed and soon proved himself as much superior to his adversary in swimming as in running. Marie dove and swam under the water as long as he could, when he rose to the surface near the Bear. He saved himself by diving and swimming in this manner several times, but his enemy followed close upon him and watched his motions with the sagacity which distinguishes these animals. At last he came up from under the water, directly beneath the jaws of the monster, which seized him by the head, the tushes piercing the scalp and neck under the right jaw and crushing the ball of his right eye. In this situation with his head in the Bear's mouth and he swimming with him ashore, St. John having heard his two shots in quick succession, came running to his rescue. St. John levelled his rifle and shot the Bear in the head, and then dragged out Marie from the water more dead than alive. I saw him six days afterwards, with a swelling on his head an inch thick, and his food and drink gushed through the opening under his jaw, made by the teeth of his terrible enemy.

We made frequent hunting excursions in small parties, in which nothing of consequence occurred. Many of us had narrow escapes from Indians and still narrower from the Grizzly and White Bears. Game became very scarce and our enemies seemed bent upon starving us out. We all became tired of this kind of life, cooped up in a small enclosure and in perpetual danger of assassination when outside the pickets. The Blackfeet manifested so determined a hatred and jealousy of our presence, that we could entertain no hope of successfully prosecuting our business, even if we could save our lives, in their country. Discouraged by the prospect before us, most of the Americans prepared to go back to the settlements, while Col. Henry and the greater part of the company, with a few Americans were getting ready to cross the mountains and go onto the Columbia beyond the vicinity of our enemies. A party which had been left at Manuel's Fort, for the purpose, had brought up one of the boats and part of the goods from the "*cache*" on the Yellow Stone below the Fort, as far as Clark's river, where, on account of the rapidity of the current, they had been compelled to leave them. Thither Menard went with men and horses to get the goods for the trip to the Columbia, and I accompanied him with most of the Americans on our way back to civilized life and the enjoyments of home. When we reached the Twenty-five Yard river we met one hundred and fifty Indians of the Gros Ventre tribe. One of the men observing a new calico shirt belonging to him, around the neck of an Indian, informed Menard of his suspicions that this party had robbed the "*cache*" (from the French, *cachee* to hide,) of the goods which they had hid in the earth near the bank of the Yellow Stone, in the fall before. Menard questioned them, but they denied the theft, saying they got the calico at the trading house. In the evening they entrenched themselves behind breastworks of logs and brush, as if fearing an attack from us, and in the morning, departed on an expedition against the snakes, of which miserable nation, we heard afterwards, they killed and took for slaves, a large number. Thus the whales of this wilderness destroy the minnows.

Here we made three canoes of buffalo bull's skins, by sewing together two skins, for each canoe, and then stretching them over a frame similar in shape to a Mackinaw boat. Our canoe contained three men, about sixty steel traps, five hundred beaver skins, our guns and amunition, besides other commodities. Nine of us started down the river in these canoes and in two days reached Clark's river where the boats with the goods was awaiting us. The rest with the horses by land. Clark's river enters the Yellow Stone from the south; near its mouth we found an army of the Crow nation encamped. This is a wandering tribe like most of the Indians in this region, without any fixed habitation. These were then at war with the Blackfeet, whom they were seeking to give battle. Having remained with us a few days, they went off towards the south. One of our hunters came into camp, on the evening of the day when they had departed, and informed us of a large force of Indians about four miles to the north, stationed behind a breast-work of rock and earth near a cliff. These were supposed to be Blackfeet, and early in the morning, the land party with the horses, having arrived, we mustered our whole force and went out to attack them in their entrenchment. We were all eager for the fight, and advancing upon them in Indian style, we discovered instead of Blackfeet, about a hundred warriors of the Crow nation, who had been out in an expedition against the Blackfeet and had just returned. They were a detachment from the army which had left us the day before. They marched into our camp on horse, two abreast, and there learning from us the news of their comrades, they immediately crossed the river in pursuit of them. Their manner of crossing the river was singular, and reminded me of the roving Tartars. They stripped themselves entirely naked, and every ten piled their accoutrements together, blankets, saddles, weapons, &c., on a tent skin made of buffalo robes, and tying it up in a large round bundle, threw it into the river and plunged after, some swimming with these huge heaps, floating like corks, and others riding the horses or holding by the tails till they had all crossed the river. Arrived on the opposite bank, which they reached in little less time than I have taken to describe their passage, they dressed, mounted their horses, and marched off two and two, as before, and were quickly out of our sight.

Here we parted from our companions, who were going to the Columbia, and who returned hence to the Forks with the goods and amunition for their trip, while we, the homeward bound, continued our course down the river in the canoes and the boat they had left, to the Fort on the Big Horn. We remained here several days, repairing a keel boat left by Manuel two years before, which we loaded with the goods from the canoes, and then recommended our descent of the Yellow Stone with the canoes and two boats. Col. Menard accompanied us in one of the boats, and I with two companions kept to our canoe in advance of the others for the purpose of killing game. On reaching the place *"cacheing"* the goods and leaving the boats, on account of the ice the year before, Menard verified his suspicions of the Gros Ventres whom he met on the Twenty-five Yard river. The pit containing the goods and effects of the men had been opened and forty trunks robbed of their contents. Another pit containing the company's goods had also been opened, and the most valuable of its store left by Menard was taken off by the Gros Ventres. They had also cut up and nearly destroyed the boats. We required one with the fragments of the other, and then passed down the river with three boats. I kept ahead as before in my skin canoe. This river is very rapid throughout its whole course, and very shallow. We were now near the Falls which are difficult and dan-

gerous of navigation. In the morning I killed two buffalos with my pistol and rifle, and my two companions
killed two more, which we up and stowed away. We approached the Falls sooner than we expected, and were
directing our course to the left side among the sunken
rocks and breakers, where we would certainly have been
lost, when we heard a gun behind and saw the men on
the boats waving us with handkerchiefs to the right. We
were barely able to gain the channel, when the canoe
shot down the descent with wonderful rapidity. We flew
along the water like a sledge down an icy hill. My two
companions lay in the bottom of the canoe, which frequently rebounded from the waves made by the rocks
under the water and stood nearly upright. The waves
washed over us and nearly filled the canoe with water.
The boats behind commenced the descent soon after we
had ended it in safety. They several times struck and
one of them hung fast on a concealed rock. We hauled
our canoe ashore, carried it above, and coming down to
the foundered boat and lighting it of part of its load, we
got it off the rocks. We now passed rapidly down to the
Missouri river, where I left my friendly canoe and went
aboard one of the boats. Here my spirits were cheered
with the near prospect of home. I longed to see the
familiar faces of kindred and friends with a yearning of
the heart, which few can realize who have not wandered
as I had done, among savages and wild beasts and made
the earth my bed and the sky my canopy for more than a
year. My way homeward was clear and comparatively
safe; the tribes along the river being friendly, or if hostile,
unable to annoy us as the Blackfeet had done so long in
the prairies.

In my wanderings in this expedition I saw much of the
Indians and their manner of living. Those in this region
were then more savage, less degraded, and more virtuous

than they are at the present time. The white man and his
"fire water" have sadly demoralized them, thinned their
numbers, and will soon sink them into oblivion. They are
no longer the proud, hauty, simple minded warriors and
orators that I found so many of them to be in 1809-10.
Sunk in poverty and intemperance, they are fast dwind-
ling away. I have seen some of the finest specimens of
men among our North American Indians. I have seen
Chiefs with the dignity of real Princes and the eloquence
of real orators, and *Braves* with the valor of the ancient
Spartans. Their manner of speaking is extremely dignified and energetic. They gesticulate with infinite grace,
freedom and animation. Their words flow deliberately,
conveying their ideas with great force and vividness of
expression, deep into the hearts of their hearers. Among
their speakers I recognized all the essentials in manner
of consumate orators. I shall have occasion, in the following chapters to bring out some of their nobler qualities
in bolder relief than was possible in the preceding, on
account of the more intimate relations I afterwards
formed with these children of nature and the prairies.

In five days after entering the Missouri, we descended
to the Gros Ventre village and our Fort, and were there
joyfully received by our old companions. Whiskey flowed
like milk and honey in the land of Canaan, being sold to
the men by the disinterested and benevolent gentlemen
of the Missouri Fur Company, for the moderate sum of
twelve dollars per gallon, they taking in payment, beaver
skins at one dollar and a half, each, which were worth in
St. Louis, six. Their prices for every thing else were in
about the same proportion. Even at this price some of the
men bought whiskey by the bucket full, and drank.

'Till they forgot their loves and debts
And cared for grief na mair.

During the carousal an incident occurred that nearly brought ruin upon us all. Three Shawnee Indians in the company from Kaskaskia, had started from the Upper Yellow Stone in a skin canoe, in advance, and had arrived a day or two before us. In their way down, one of them named Placota had wantonly killed a Crow Indian on the Yellow Stone, and a Gros Ventre on the Missouri, about sixty miles above the village, and taken their scalps. In his drunken fit Placota brought out one of these scalps in full view of the friendly Gros Ventres. Menard caught it out of his hand and hid it from view. The Indians became greatly excited, crowded around us and demanded to know whose scalp it was. Menard then produced to them the scalp of the Indian whom Cheek had killed and which they had seen before. They said this was a "dry" and the other a "green" scalp. We at last, and with great difficulty, pacified them and quieted their suspicions. Placota, who was raging mad, by Menard's orders was tied behind the trading house till he became sober, when I released him on his promise of good behavior.

This tribe was then very powerful, having in all five villages, and mustering, in case of emergency, as many as three thousand warriors. I have already noticed their character and warlike qualities. A singular custom prevails among them in cutting off a finger or inflicting a severe wound in remembrance of any severe misfortune. Few of the men thirty years of age, were without the marks of these wounds, made on the death of some near relation or on occasion of a defeat of the nation in war. Some I saw with three and one with four fingers cut off. I saw a young man bewailing the death of his father in a battle with the Blackfeet. He had compelled his friends to draw leather cords through the flesh under his arms and on his back, and attaching three Buffalo skulls, weighing at least twenty-five pounds, to the ends of the cords he dragged them over the ground after him through the village, moaning and lamenting in great distress. At their meals, the Indians on the Missouri, throw the first piece of meat in the direction of an absent friend. In smoking, they send the first whiff upwards in honor of the Great Spirit, the second downward as a tribute to their great mother, the third to the right and the fourth to the left, in thanks to the Great Spirit for the game. He sends them so abundantly on the bosom of the earth. Their name for Chief is *Inca*, the same as that of the South American and Mexican Indians. For knife they say *messa;* for horses, *cowalla.* A comparison of their languages will show an identity in their origin and race. They secure their dead by setting four poles, forked at the top, and about twenty-five feet in height, in the ground. On these they put a scaffold of buffalo skin, fastened to the poles, and on this the corpse is placed, covered by a buffalo skin bound around it very tightly. In this way the corpse is protected from the birds and beasts, and thus it remains till the scaffold falls by decay. The bones are then gathered by the relatives and put into a common heap. I saw in the rear of the Gros Ventre village an immense extent of ground covered by these tombs in the air, and near by was a heap of skulls and bones which had fallen to the earth from these air graves.

After a few day's stay at the Fort and village, we again started down the river with Col. Menard and two boats. We arrived at St. Louis in the month of August, A. D. 1810, without any occurrence of interest on the voyage. We never got our dues or any thing of the least similitude to justice from the company. They brought me in their debt two hundred dollars, and some of the other Americans, for still larger sums. The reader may ask how this could be. He can easily imagine the process when he is told that the company charged us six dollars per pound for powder, three dollars for lead, six dollars for coarse calico shirts, one dollar and a half per yard for coarse tow linen for tents, the same for a common butcher knife, and so on, and allowed us only what I have mentioned for our beaver skins, our only means of payment. Capt. Lewis told me not to lay in any supplies in St. Louis, as the Company had plenty and could sell them to me as cheaply as I could get them in St. Louis, or nearly so, allowing only for a reasonable profit. Lewis did not intend to deceive us and was chagrined at the villanous conduct of the Company afterwards. This, with the fraudulent violation of their contracts and promises in the Indian country, by this concern, makes up a piece of extortion, fraud and swindling, that ought to consign the parties engaged in it to eternal infamy. The heaviest blame must rest on the unprincipled Liza; but the rest of the company must suffer the stigma of having connived at and profited by the villainy, if they did not actually originate and urge it onward. I sued them on my contract, and was the only one who did so. After many delays and continuances from term to term, I was glad to get rid of the suits and them, by giving my note for one hundred dollars to the Company. This, with my debt to Colter, made me a loser to the amount of three hundred dollars by one years trapping on the head waters of the Missouri. Some of the Americans, however, fared much worse, and were deterred from returning to the settlements at all, by their debts to the Company, which they were hopeless of discharging by any ordinary business in which they could engage. Such is one instance of the kind and considerate justice of wealth, to defenceless poverty, beautifully illustrating the truth of the sentiment uttered by somebody, "take care of the rich and the rich will take care of the poor."

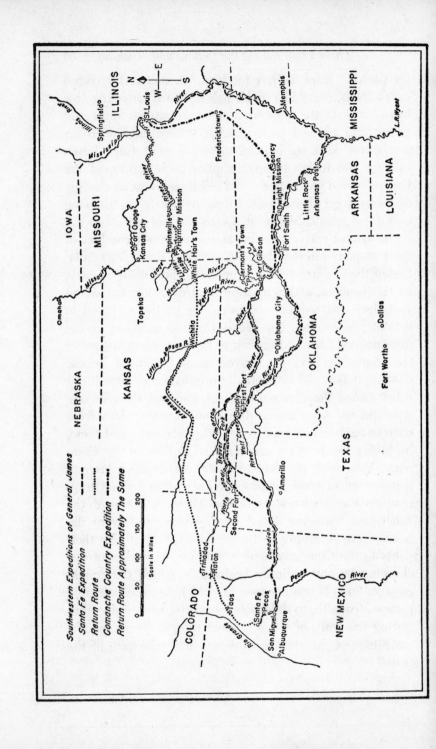

CHAPTER III

Employment from 1810 to 1821—The First Santa Fe Traders—
Members of the Fourth Santa Fe expedition—Ascent of the
Arkansas—Vaugean—Removal of the Town of Little Rock—Fort
Smith and Major Bradford—Trading with the Osages—Capt.
Prior—Salt River—Salt Plains and Shining Mountains—Robbery
by the Indians—Sufferings from thirst—Attack by the Indians—
Further Robberies—The One Eyed Chief and Big Star—Indian
Council—Critical Situation—Rescue by Spanish officers—Cordaro
Journey continued—San Miguil Peccas and its Indian inhabi-
tants—Santa Fe—Farming.

AFTER MY RETURN from the Upper Missouri, I went in the
fall of 1810 to Pennsylvania, where I remained two years
and married. I returned to St. Louis, in the fall of 1813,
procured a keel-boat and with it, navigated the Ohio and
Mississippi, between Pittsburgh and St. Louis, carrying
goods for large profits. I continued in this business till the
fall of 1815, when I took a stock of goods from McKnight
& Brady of St. Louis, and opened a store in Harrisonville,
Illinois, dividing profits equally among us. In the fall of
1818, I went to Baltimore with letters of recommendation
and bought goods for cash and on credit to the amount of
seventeen thousand dollars, and brought them in waggons
to Pittsburgh where I left them to await a rise of the
river, which was too low for navigation, and came to
St. Louis. My goods were not sent on till the following
spring, when they had greatly fallen in price and the
market was filled with a large supply. I was unable to
dispose of my stock even at cost. I struggled on through

the years 1819,-'20, with the certain prospect of bank-ruptcy before my face, amid the clamors of creditors, and without the hope of extricating myself from impending ruin. About this time Baum, Beard, and Chambers, with some others, came to St. Louis from Santa Fe, where they had been imprisoned by the Government ever since the year 1810. They, with Robert, brother of John McKnight of the firm of McKnight and Brady, and eight others, were the first American Santa Fe traders that carried goods from St. Louis to New Mexico. Immediately on reaching Santa Fe their goods were confiscated by the Governor, sold at public auction, and themselves taken to Chihuahua and there thrown into prison, where they were kept in more or less strict confinement for the space of ten years, being supported during that time by the proceeds of McKnight's goods, the Government allowing 18¾ cents per day to each man. This, I believe was the second com-pany of Americans that ever entered Santa Fe. Clem. Morgan, a Portuguese and very wealthy, made his way thither at a very early day, while Louisiana belonged to Spain, and returned in safety, making a good venture. Gen. Zebulon Pike was the first American visitor to that coun-try. He went in the year 1807, and on his arrival was marched through Mexico as a prisoner of war, but was soon after released on demand of our Government. One of his men was detained thirteen years by the Spaniards, and returned with Chambers to St. Louis. Pike in the beginning of our last war with England, met a soldier's death at Queenston Heights. The second company from the United States was McKnight's and their treatment has been noticed. The third was under the command of Augustus Chouteau and Demun of St. Louis, and was composed entirely of French. They made a very unsuc-cessful venture, being deprived of their goods worth $40,000, without the least remuneration, and themselves imprisoned for a short time. I commanded the fourth expedition to Santa Fe from the United States, and the first that was made after the Mexican Revolution and the declaration of their independence on Spain, and I was the first American that ever visited the country and escaped a prison while there. John McKnight desired to go to Mexico to see his brother, procure his release if he were still in prison, and return with him to the States. The first information he had received, concerning Robert, in ten years, came by his companions above named, who had left him in the interior of Mexico. He proposed that I should take my goods and accompany him, and supposed that under Spanish protection we could go unmolested by the Government. The news of the Revolution had not yet reached this country. This appeared to be the best course to retrieve my affairs, and I prepared for the journey by procuring a passport from Don Onis the Spanish Minister, countersigned by John Q. Adams, then Secretary of State under Monroe. I loaded a keel-boat with goods to the value of $10,000, and laid in a large quantity of biscuit, whiskey, flour, lead and powder, for trading with the Indians on the route. I started from St. Louis on the tenth of May, A. D. 1821, and descended the Mississippi to the mouth of the Arkansas. The company consisted, besides myself, of McKnight, my brother John G. James, David Kirkee, Wm. Shearer, Alexander Howard, Benjamin Potter, John Ivy, and Francois Maesaw, a Spaniard. Two joined us after starting, Frederick Hector at the mouth of the Ohio, and James Wilson in the Cherokee country, making eleven in all, young and daring men, eager for excitement and adventure. Ascending the Arkansas, the first settlement we reached was "Eau Post," inhabited principally by French. A few days afterwards we arrived in the country of the Quawpaws, where we met with a Frenchman named Veaugean, an old man of considerable wealth, who treated us with hospitality. His son had just returned from hunting with a party of Quawpaws and had been attacked by the Pawnees, who killed several of his Indian companions. Pawnee was then the name of all the tribes that are now known as Camanches. I had never known or heard of any Indians of that name before I visited their country on my way to Santa Fe. The Americans previously knew them only as Pawnees. The account brought by Veaugean's son surprised me, as we had heard that all the Indians on our route were friendly. Leaving Veaugean's, we proceeded up the river through a very fertile country. Dense and heavy woods of valuable timber lined both sides of the river, both below "Eau Post" and above as far as we went, and the river bottoms, which are large, were covered by extensive cane-brakes, which appeared impenetrable even by the rattlesnake. Small fields of corn, squash and pumpkins, cultivated by Indians, appeared in view on the low banks of the river. Since entering the Arkansas we had found the country quite level; after sailing and pushing about three hundred miles from the mouth, we now reached the first high land, near Little Rock the capital of the Territory as established that spring. The archives had not yet been removed from Eau Post, the former capital. As we approached Little Rock we beheld a scene of true Western life and character, that no other country could present. First we saw a large wood and stone building in flames, and then about one hundred men, painted, masked and disguised in almost every conceivable manner, engaged in removing the Town. These men, with ropes and chains would march off a frame house on wheels and logs, place it about three or four hundred yards from its former site and then return and move off another in the same manner. They all seemed tolerably drunk, and among them I recognized almost every European language spoken. They were a jolly set indeed. Thus they worked amid songs and shouts, until by night-fall they had completely changed the site of their Town. Such buildings as they could not move they burned down, without a dissentant voice. The occasion of this strange proceeding was as follows: The Territorial Court was then in session at Diamond Hill, about thirty miles distant on the river above, and the news had reached Little Rock on the morning of our arrival, that a suit pending in this Court and involving the title to the town, wherein one Russell of St. Louis was the claimant, had gone against the citizens of Little Rock and in favor of Russell. The whole community instantly turned out en masse and in one day and night Mr. Russell's land was disencumbered of the Town of Little Rock. They coolly and quietly, though not without much unnecessary noise, took the Town up and set it down on a neighboring claim of the Quawpaw tribe, and fire removed what was irremovable in a more convenient way. The free and enlightened citizens of Little Rock made a change of Landlords more rapidly than Bonaparte took Moscow. Here I saw Matthew Lyon, then quite an old man, canvassing for Congress. He was a man of some note in John Adam's administration, by whom he was imprisoned, under the Alien and Sedition law. He came into Little Rock, with the Judge and Lawyers, from Diamond Hill, the day after the grand moving of the Town. He rode a mule, which had thrown him into a bayou, and his appearance as he came in, covered with mud from head to foot, was a subject of much laughter for his companions and the town of Little Rock, which had now began to assume a look of some age, being just twenty-four hours old. Lyon was not returned to Congress and he died a few years afterwards. In 1824 I saw his grave at Spadre, in the Cherokee country, where he had kept a trading establishment. Before I left Little Rock I procured a license to trade with all the Indian tribes on the Arkansas and its tributaries, from Secretary Charles Crittenden, Governor Miller being out of the Territory. I gave bond in the sum of $3000, with Judge Scott as security, to observe the laws of the United States, and it always appeared to me that I was entitled to indemnity from my country for the robberies which I suffered from the Indians. My losses in this way were tremendous and have weighed me down to the earth from that day to this, the best portion of my life; but not one cent have I ever been able to obtain from the justice of Congress, whose laws I was bound to obey, whose license from the hands of a Government officer I carried with me, and who by every rule of justice was bound to protect me in a business which it authorized by license and regulated by heavy penalties.

Continuing our course up the river, we passed through a more rocky and uneven country than that below Little Rock. The Maumel mountain, some fifty or sixty miles above this Town, and a mile from the south bank of the river, is a great curiosity. It rises six hundred feet above the level of the river, and in shape resembles a coal-pint. A large spring of fresh water gushes from the top and runs down its side to the river. We now passed through the country of the Cherokees, whose farms and log houses made a fine appearance on the banks of the river, and would compare favorably with those of any western State. They were at this time highly civilized and have since made great advances in the arts. These were that part of the nation called the Rogers party, who just emigrated from the east to the west side of the Mississippi, and utimately, about the year 1833, with the powerful agency of the General Government, caused the removal of the whole nation to this country, where they are making rapid progress in national prosperity. Their Delegate will take his seat in our next Congress as Representative of the first

Indian Territory ever organized. If this nation shall form a nucleus for the preservation of the race from annihilation, the cheerless predictions of the Physiologists will be most fortunately falsified, and the Philanthropist will rejoice in the perpetuation of the true Indian race and character.

Fort Smith lies about six hundred miles from the mouth of the Arkansas on the western confines of the Cherokee country, and near that of the Osages, which tribes were now at war with each other. We stopped a few days at this post, where we were well received by Lieutenant Scott and the commandant Major Bradford, who examined and approved our license. The Major was a small stern looking man, an excellent disciplinarian and a gallant officer. He invited McKnight and me to make his house our home until we had rested our company and put our guns in good order preparatory to entering the Indian country. He and his wife treated us with the utmost kindness and hospitality, and on leaving, presented us a large supply of garden vegetables, with a barrel of onions, which we were not to broach until we had killed our first buffalo, when we were enjoined to have "a general feast in honor of old Billy Bradford." His kindness made a deep impression on us. We here tried to mark out our course for the future, which we determined should be the Arkansas to within sixty miles Loas in New Mexico, Baum having told me that this river was navigable thus far, and the Canadian being two shallow for our boat. Parting from the hospitable old Major, we ascended the river to the Salt Fork, which enters from the south, passing in our way the Grand River, then called the Six Bulls, and the Verdigris, at whose mouth Fort Gibson has since been built. The waters of the Salt Fork are very much saturated with salt, tasting like strong brine where they enter the Arkansas. After this we proceeded with great difficulty, and about thirty miles above the South Fork our further progress was entirely stopped by the lowness of the water. There being no prospect of a speedy rise in the river at this time, which was the mouth of August, we returned four miles to an Osage road, which we had observed in going up, and here I sent three men to the Osage village, which I knew could not be far distant, for the purpose of opening a trade with this tribe. In five or six days these men returned to me with forty Osages and a Capt. Prior, formerly of the United States army. I mentioned him in the first chapter as the commander of the escort of the Mandan Chief Shehaka. He was a Sergeant in Lewis and Clark's expedition, and a Captain at the battle of New Orleans. On the reduction of the army after the war, he was discharged to make way for some parlor soldier and sunshine patriot, and turned out in his old age upon the "world's wide common." I found him here among the Osages, with whom he had taken refuge from his country's ingratitude, and was living as one of their tribe, where he may yet be unless death has discharged the debt his country owed him.

I took out some goods, and with McKnight, my brother, and the Spaniard Macsaw, accompanied Capt. Prior and the Indians to their village, to the south east, which we reached in two days. Here we found our old friend, Maj. Bradford Hugh Glenn, from Cincinnati, with goods and about twenty men, on his way to the Spanish country, and also, Capt. Barbour, and Indian trader from the mouth of the Verdigris, and formerly of Pittsburgh. I proposed to Glenn, whom I shall have to mention unfavorably hereafter, to travel in company to the Spanish country; but he appearing averse to the arrangement, I did not urge it upon him. I bought twenty-three horses of the Osages at high prices, for packing my goods, and agreed with Barbour to "*cache*" (hide in the earth) my heaviest and

least portable goods near the Arkansas, for him to take
in the following spring down to his store at the mouth of
the Verdigris, sell them and account to me for the proceeds on my return. I returned with my companions to
the river and carefully concealed my flour, whiskey, lead,
hardware and other heavy goods. I showed Capt. Prior,
who came up the next day with a party of Osages going
out on their fall hunt, the place where I had hid these
goods, and packing the rest on my horses, we left the
Arkansas to our right, or the north, and travelled with
Prior and the Indians for two days toward the south-west.
We then left them and bore directly to the west in the
direction as pointed out to us by the Indians, of the Salt
Plains and Shining Mountains. In eleven days we struck
the Salt Fork, mentioned before, and which is set down
on the latest maps as the Cinnamon river. In the distance
before us we discerned the bright mountains before mentioned, which the Indians had directed us to pass in our
route. We held on our course for two days along the right
bank of the Salt Fork, over mounds and between hills of
sand which the wind had blown up in some place to the
height of one hundred feet. Our progress was very slow,
the horses sometimes siking to their breasts in the sand.
The bed of the river in many places was quite dry, the
water being lost in the sand, and as we advanced, it appeared covered over with salt, like snow. The water,
mantled over with salt, stood in frequent pools, from the
bottom of which we could scoop up that mineral in
bushels. The channel of the Salt river became narrower
and more shallow as we proceeded. The sand so obstructed
our progress that we crossed the river where traveling was
less difficult, and soon struck a branch of the Salt Fork,
equally impregnated with salt as the main stream. Large
crusts of salt lay at the water's edge. Proceeding on we
came to the Shining Mountains, and a high hill evidently

based upon salt. It stands near the salt branch, the banks of which were composed of salt rocks, from which the men broke off large pieces with their tomahawks. Here, and in the Salt river was enough of this valuable mineral to supply the world for an indefinite period. The Shining Mountains lay south of us about four miles and had been visible for several days. We visited them and found one of the greatest curiosities in our country. I have never seen them nor the salt plains in which they stand put down on any map or described by any white man. All of our travellers in this region appear to have passed to the north or south of them, as I have never seen or heard of a description of them, except by the Indians, who come here regularly and in great force, for salt. The mountains stand separate from each other, are about three hundred feet in height, and are quite flat on the summit. They are composed, in part, of a shining semi-transparent rock, which reflects the rays of the sun to a great distance. It is soft, being easily cut with a knife, and the hand is visible through thin pieces of it when held in the sun light. They extend about thirty miles on the left of Salt river in a north-west and south-east direction, are all of an equal height, containing an area on the top of from ten rods to a hundred acres, and are entirely destitute of timber. The tops of most of them were inaccessible. With great difficulty we ascended one of about ten acres in extent, from which we saw along the tops of the others, they all being on the same plane. We found the short thin grass of the prairie below, but no shrub except the prickly pear. The ground was covered with immense quantities of buffalo manure, when left there it would be vain to conjecture. The substance from the ground was clay for upwards of two hundred feet, then came the rock from ten to twenty feet thick, projecting over the earth, and the soil above was about ten feet in depth. The rock is fast crumbling away by the action of water, which seems to dissolve it, as we found very few fragments at the foot of the mountains and none of any considerable size. The whole country was evidently at one time, on a level with these singular elevations.

We continued our course up the bank of the same branch of Salt river by which we had come. Its water was now, after leaving the salt plains, fresh and wholesome, and we travelled along its bank two days, when finding it took us too much to the north, we left it and bore to the southwest. This was the sixth day after reaching the Salt Fork, and seventeen after parting with Capt. Prior and the Osages. We killed seven buffalo after leaving the Shining Mountains, and dried the meat. The carcasses of the buffaloes attracting the buzzards with some old shoes and other small articles left on the ground by the men, served to discover us to a war party of Camanches who were now on our trail. After leaving the Salt Branch we travelled till near night without finding wood or water, and then bore again to the north-west till we struck the Branch. We cooked our meat with fuel of buffalo manure which we gathered for the purpose. Towards morning we were all alarmed by the barking of our dogs, followed by a clapping noise and the sound of footsteps. We slept no more on that night, and in the morning saw upwards of a hundred Indians at a short distance coming with the design of intercepting our horses, which were some distance from the camp. One horse was pierced by a lance. I exhibited the flag, which diverted their course, and they came among us in a very hostile manner, seizing whatever they could lay their hands on. The interpreter told us they were a war party and advised me to make peace with them by giving them presents. I did so, distributing about three thousand dollars worth of goods among them. There were two Chiefs in this party, one of whom was friendly and the other, called the one-eyed Chief, seemed determined to take our lives. His party, however, was in a minority and soon after went off. The friendly Chief then came up to me and on account of his interference in our behalf demanded more presents, which I made to him. He told me that if I came to the village I should be well treated and implored me not to go up the Arkansas. I afterwards learned that the one-eyed Chief had left me with the purpose of waylaying us on that river and taking our lives, which was the reason of the friendly Chief's advice. Those who were hostile, and they were the whole of the one-eyed Chief's party, seemed perfectly enfuriated against us. They scrutinized our equipments, said we had Osage horses and were spies of that nation, with whom they were then at war. At last we were rid of the presence of these unpleasant visitors with many dismal apprehensions for the future. The friendly Chief left a Mexican Indian, an interpreter, with us as a guide. With him we struck from the south branch of Salt river, for the north Fork of the Canadian, which the Indians told us we should reach in one day's travel. Going in a direction west of south we struck the river on the second day, having suffered dreadfully for want of water. McKnight and I went forward to find water and killed a buffalo. We drank large draughts of the blood of this animal, which I recollect tasted like milk. We found several ponds of water, so tainted with buffalo manure as to cause us to vomit on drinking of it. We missed the party on that night and found them on the next day, all sick from the water they had drunk, and exhausted by previous fatigue and thirst. The horses were nearly worn out by the same causes. We travelled along the North Fork of the Canadian for seven or eight days, until we reached its head in a large morass, or swamp, about two miles wide, and five or six long, situate in a valley which gradually narrows and disappears at last in the vast plain to the west. We went up this valley which was now dry, but in the spring is filled with a rapid stream. We saw thousands of buffalo along its course, and found a large pond about an acre in extent, but the water was so spoiled by manure, as to sicken us all. After passing through this valley we bore for the Canadian river towards the south, and on the second day, after intense suffering from thirst, we struck a fine spring of fresh water. This was a rich source of real refreshment and enjoyment. Following the stream made by this spring we reached the Canadian, and travelled up its course for several days. We had encamped for the night on the twenty-first day after meeting the Camanches who had robbed us on the branch of Salt river, when we saw a great number of mounted Indians coming over a rising ground in our front, and at their head the friendly Chief, who advanced with outstretched hands crying *towauc, towaue,*—"good, good." Coming up he embraced me in Indian custom, and requested me to go with him to his village. Here an Indian seized a brass kettle and rode off with it. This act alarmed me, and I asked the Chief if he could protect my property if I went with him. He said he could not, and I declined his invitation for that night, and requested him to leave a body of trusty Indians, to defend me till morning. He did so, and we were not molested that night. In the morning we marched with our guard from the left bank of the river, where we had encamped, to the right bank, and in two miles above we found the whole village of the Indians, numbering a thousand lodges, situated in the bottom near the base of a large mound. We were met by one of the principal Chiefs, whose looks were to me ominous of evil. He was a little vicious looking old man and eyed me most maliciously. We were taken close to the foot of the mound near this Chief's lodge, and there we encamped, having piled up my goods and covered them with skins. The Indians then demanded presents and about a thousand chiefs and warriors surrounded us. I laid out for them tobacco, powder, lead, vermillion, calico, and other articles, amounting to about $1,000 in value. This did not satisfy them, and they began to break open my bales of cloth and divide my finest woolens designed for the Spanish market, among them. After losing about $1000 more in this way, I induced them to desist from further robbery. The principal chief named Big Star, now appeared and said they had enough. They divided the spoil among two or three thousand, of whom all got some. They tore up the cloth into garments for the middle and blankets. They tied the silk handkerchiefs to their hair as ornaments, which streamed in the wind. This robbery over, I smoked with them and prepared to go on my journey. This they forbade and we were compelled to stay over that day. We kept a strong guard through the night on our goods and horses. On the next morning they pretended that another party had arrived who required presents. This information was brought by a one-eyed Spaniard, who acted as interpreter and had got from me as a present, a whole suit of cloth and a large supply of amunition. He was the instigator of this new demand. The Indians began to gather around us, and break open and drag about the goods. The Chiefs stood off, taking no part. I then made them another set of presents, worth, probably, a thousand dollars more. We now hoped to be allowed to pass on, and requested leave to go, but they refused it; and the friendly chief advised us to stay. I had seen many savages, but none so suspicious and little as these. They seemed to regard us as spies in their country. We staid with them the second day and night without any further robbery than that I have mentioned. On the third day of my stay, the one-eyed Chief came into the village from the Arkansas, where he had been, with a hundred men, awaiting us with murderous designs. On his coming in, the interpreter, Maesaw, ran to me, saying we should certainly be killed, and the woman and children ran from their lodges like chickens before a hawk. I had made the Big Star Chief my friend by presenting him with a splendid sword. He now came up and took me into the little old Chief's lodge, saying I would be shot if I remained out. Our time seemed nearly come. In the distance we saw the one-eyed with his troop approaching, all painted black and armed with guns, bows and arrows and lances. We were eleven against a hundred at least, perhaps thousands. The Big Star sent a messenger to my enemy and asked him what would satisfy him in lieu of our lives. He replied that he must have for each of his men as much cloth as his outstretched arms would once measure; an equal quantity of calico; powder, lead, vermillion, knives, beads, looking glasses, &c., and for himself the sword which he had seen on the south branch of Salt river. I sent him word that I had not the vermillion, knives, beads and looking glasses, nor the sword, which I had presented to the Big Star. He said the story about the sword was a lie, that I had given it to Big Star to prevent him from getting it, and that he would have it or my scalp, and as to the other articles he would take cloth instead of them. The Big Star here sent to his lodge for the sword, and taking it in his hand, he pressed its side to his heart and then handed it to me, saying, "take it and send it to the one-eyed Chief. You have no other way of saving your life and the lives of your people." I did as he advised, and measured off about five hundred yards of cloth and calicoe, of which the former cost me seven dollars per yard in Baltimore, and sent them to my deadly enemy. This appeared to pacify him and again I proposed to go on my way. To this they again objected, saying that the whole village would go down the river in the morning, and we should then be permitted to part from them and continue our course up the river as before meeting with them. We had the horses brought up, and prepared, that evening, for an early start in the morning. One half kept guard while the rest of our party endeavored to sleep. But there was no rest for any of us on that most dismal night. This was the third sleepless night which we had passed with these ferocious savages, and we were nearly worn down by fatigue, anxiety and watching. Before day-light a party of boys ascended the mound in our rear, and from the top stoned our company until they were dislodged and driven down by the exertions of the friendly Chief. Uncertain of our fate and nearly exhausted, we awaited in sullen patience, the issue of events. The sun as he rose seemed to wear an aspect of gloom, and every thing portended evil to our little band. Six of my horses had been taken in the night, and I ordered my men out to find and bring them back. The friendly Chief now came to me with great concern and dejection in his countenance, and begged of me not to leave my station or allow the men to go out.

"Keep together," said he, "or you will be killed. The men that go out will be murdered. Don't try to get back your horses." I saw that the whole army were preparing to decamp, and pulling down their lodges. Sometime after sunrise, I perceived about fifty of the Chiefs and older Indians going up unto the mound above us, in our rear, followed by a multitude of young warriors and boys. An old man turned and drove them back: the two friendly Chiefs did not go up. Arrived at the top, this company formed the circle, sat down and smoked. Then one of their number commenced what seemed to us, from his gestures, to be a violent harangue, designed to inflame their passions. I told my company that this council would decide our fate. They asked me how I knew this. If they come down, said I, friendly, we shall have nothing to fear; but if sulky, and out of humor, we have nothing to hope. Put your guns in good order, and be prepared for the worst. We must sell our lives as dearly as possible. In this sentiment they all agreed with me, and we prepared to meet our fate, whatever it should be, like men. During this time, the lodges, with the women and children, were fast disappearing, and the men assembling before us on horseback and afoot, armed with guns, bows, and lances. The council on the hill, after an hour's consultation, descended, and we soon learned that our deaths were determined upon. Those Indians who before were sociable, were now distant and sulky. When spoken to by any of us they made no answer.

The friendly Chief and Big Star, who had taken no part in the council, now came and shook hands, and bade us farewell. I besought them to stay with us; shaking their heads sorrowfully, they went away. The press in front now greatly increased. Nearly two thousand warriors stood before and around us, with the evident intention of making an attack, and appeared to be waiting the signal for the onslaught. We stood in a circle with our backs to the goods and saddles heaped up above all our heads; and with our rifles raised to our breasts, and our fingers on the triggers. We were also armed with knives and tomahawks. Old Jemmy Wilson seized an axe, having no gun, and swore he would hew his way as far as he could. Thus we stood eleven against two thousand, with death staring us in the face. All seemed unwilling to commence the bloody work. The suspense was awful. I stood between John McKnight and my brother, and noticed their countenances. McKnight's face was white, and his chin and lips were quivering. My brother, as brave a man as ever lived, looked desperate and de-

termined. Not a man but seemed bent to die in arms
and fighting, and none were overcome by fear.

Thus we stood near half an hour in deathly silence;
at length the White Bear warrior, a Chief dressed in a
whole Bear skin, with the claws hanging over his hands,
rode swiftly towards us, through the crowd, with his
lance in his hand, as if to annihilate us at once; but
seeing the dangerous position he was in, he stopped
short about five paces from us, and glared upon me with
the most deadly malignity. Finding he could not reach
me with his lance, he took out his pistol, examined the
priming, tossed out the powder from the pan, re-primed,
and again fixed his devilish eyes full upon me. But he
saw that I could fire first, and he kept his pistol down.
Here McKnight first broke the dreadful silence, saying,
"let us commence James, you will be the first one killed—
this suspense is worse than death; the black Chief is my
mark." I said no, McKnight, let us forbear as long as
they do; for us to begin is folly in the extreme; but as
soon as a gun is fired, we must fire, rush in and sell our
lives as dearly as possible. Here Kirker walked out with
his gun over his head, gave it up, and passed into the
crowd unmolested. In a minute afterwards we heard a
cry from a distance, approaching nearer and nearer, of
Tabbaho, Tabbaho.* This I supposed was on account of
Kirker's surrender. The cry increased and spread throughout the crowd. Looking towards the south-west, whence
the cry arose, while the While Bear's attention was with-
drawn, I saw six horsemen riding at full speed, and as
they came nearer, we heard the words in Spanish, save
them! save them! In a moment a Spanish officer rushed
into our arms, exclaiming, thank God we are in time;
you are all safe and unhurt. He said that he had heard of
our danger by accident, that morning, and ridden twenty

* White men.

miles to save us. All the circumstances of our rescue we
learned the next day. With joyous and thankful hearts
for our escape from a death that, five minutes before
seemed inevitable, we prepared to depart with our pre-
servers. I had bidden farewell, as I thought forever, to
my wife, child, home and all its endearments, and the
thoughts of them were now overpowering to me. The
Spaniards asked the Indians why they were going to
kill us. They answered, that the Spanish governor at
Santa Fe had commanded them not to let any American
pass, but that we were determined to go in spite of them,
so that to stop us and keep their promise to the Spanish
Governor, they thought they were compelled to take
our lives. The Spaniards told them that this was under
the government of Spain, but that they were now independent and free, and brothers to the Americans. This
was the first news I had heard of the Mexican revolution.

The two friendly Chiefs now returned, and I showed
the Spaniards our passport. The Indians brought in and
delivered up four of my horses. The whole village, soon
after the arrival of the Spaniards, went down the river;
and our party, except Maesaw and myself, with two of
the Spanish officers, started forward towards the Spanish
camp, about twenty miles distant. We four remained behind to recover the two missing horses, and then followed our companions. We were lost, at dark, among the
cliffs bordering the river, where we made fire for cooking
our suppers, and encamped for the night. Early the next
morning we reached the Spanish encampment, where
our party was awaiting us. As we approached the camp
there came out to meet us, a tall Indian of about seventy
years of age, dressed in the complete regimentals of
an American Colonel, with blue coat, red sash, white
pantaloons, epaulets and sword. He advanced with an
erect, military air and saluted us with great dignity and

address. His eyes were still bright and piercing, un-dimmed in the least by age, and he had a high, noble forehead and Roman nose. His whole port and air struck me forcibly as those of a real commander and a hero. After saluting us he handed me a paper which I read as follows, as nearly as I now remember.

This is to certify that Cordaro, a Chief of the Camanches, has visited the Fort at Nacotoche with fifteen of his tribe; that he remained here two weeks, and during the whole time be-haved very well. It is my request that all Americans who meet him or any of his tribe, should treat him and them with great respect and kindness, as they are true friends of the United States.

JOHN JAMESON
U. S. Indian Agent at Nacotoche on Red River

This Chief, Cordaro, was the cause of our being then in existence. He told us he had promised his "great friend at Nacotoche" that he would protect all Americans that came through his country, and he very earnestly re-quested us to inform his "great friend" that he had been as good as his word. On entering the encampment, we found about fifty Spaniards and three hundred Caman-che warriors, who had just returned from an expedition against the Navahoes, a tribe inhabiting the country west of Santa Fe and the mountains, and who were then at war with the Spaniards. On their return from this cam-paign this party had come from Santa Fe with their Ca-manche allies into their country to hunt for buffalo and had encamped the night before our rescue from the Ca-manches, on the spot where we now found them. On the next morning a party of Indians belong to this band were hunting their horses in the prairie and met another party from the army below, who had us in custody, en-gaged in the same manner, who informed them that their countrymen had taken a company of Americans prisoners,

and were going to kill them all that morning, and divide
their goods among the army; that the whole village was
breaking up and preparing to go down the Canadian,
and that the pulling down of the last lodge was to be the
signal for our massacre. On hearing this the first party
hastened back to their camp with the news which brought
out most of the young warriors to come down for a share
of the plunder of my goods. The Chief Cordaro went instantly, on hearing this account, to the Spanish officers,
told them that a company of Americans were to be murdered that morning by his countrymen, mentioned the
signal for the attack, said he was too old to ride fast,
or he would go himself to the rescue, and adjured them
to mount and ride without sparing the horses, as not a
moment was to be lost. Six of them mounted and rode
as Cordaro had told them to do, and we saw their foam-
ing steeds and heard the cry of *Tabbaho*—(*white men*)—
just in time to save us from extermination. A minute after
would probably have been too late. Our determined attitude averted the blow and prolongued our time to the
last moment, when our deliverers appeared; but without
them, the next instant would have seen a volley of shot
and arrows lay most of us low and the lance and tomahawk would have soon completed the work on us all.

—Cordaro, the noble and true hearted savage, appeared
to rejoice at our escape as much as we. He desired particularly that his "great friend" at Nacotoche should hear
of his agency in saving us, and I had to promise him
repeatedly that I would surely inform Col. Jameson when
I saw him, of the manner in which his friend, Cordaro,
had performed his promise to him. If John Jameson be
still alive and this page meet his eye, I shall have cause
to felicitate myself in having at last kept my word to
my Camanche preserver.

We spent that day with Cordaro and the Spaniards,

and held a council or "talk" with them. Cordaro made a speech dissuading me from going to Santa Fe on account of the treatment which the Americans had always received from the Government there. "They will imprison you," said he to me, "as they have imprisoned all Americans that ever went to Santa Fe. You will meet the fate of all your countrymen before you." The Spanish officers, who were all present at this harangue, smiled and said there was no danger of any ill-treatment to us, now that they had an independent government. Cordaro shook his head increduously, and told them that we were under his protection; that he would himself go to Sante Fe after we had arrived there, and if he found us imprisoned, he would immediately go to war with them. "The Americans are my friends," said he, "and I will not permit them to be hurt. I have promised my great friend of Nacotoche to protect all Americans that come through my country." The Spaniards promised to treat us well, but our protector seemed to be very suspicious of them and evidently gave little faith to their promises. We found at this camp an excellent Spanish interpreter, who spoke the Camanche language as well as his own. By him I was informed that the Indians took me for the Frenchman Vaugean, whom we had seen in the country of the Quawpaws, a tribe of kin to the Osages, and who, while hunting on the Canadian in the spring before with a party of thirty French and Indians of the former tribe, had been attacked by the Camanches, who were defeated and driven back with considerable loss. Vaugean, like myself, was a tall man, and the Indians here and those we had met before, considered me the commander in this battle. The one-eyed interpreter had concealed this fact from me, and we now had some difficulty in satisfying the Indians that we were not the same party who with Vaugean, were in alliance with their enemies, the Osages. The charge was frequently renewed, but we at last succeeded in repelling it and quieting their suspicions. On the next day, the third day after meeting with the Spanish officers, we parted with Cordero who followed his countrymen down the Canadian, with the Spanish force in his company. Two of the Spanish officers remained to accompany us to Santa Fe. They were all very gentlemanly and liberal minded men. One Spanish citizen of Santa Fe had hired to return with me as a guide. We once more took up our march along the Canadian and over the immense plains by the trail of the Spaniards we had just parted with. The whole country here is one immense prairie. I observed many huge granite rocks standing like stone buildings, some of them, one hundred feet high. The earth seemed to have been washed from around them and the prairies below to have been formed by deposits of earth and crumbled rocks from these and similar elevations. Some were covered with earth and cedar trees, but most of them were entirely bare. In three days after leaving Cordaro we came in sight of the Rocky Mountains, whose three principal peaks, covered with perpetual snow were glittering in the sun. The most northern and highest of these peaks is set down on the latest map I have seen as "James' Peak or Pike's." Gen. Pike endeavored to reach its top, but without success. After my return I made a rough map with a pen, of this country, for the use of Senator Kane of Illinois, and in the next map published by Government, I saw my name affixed to this peak, as I supposed, by the agency of Mr. Kane. The peak bore no name known to our company when we saw it and I gave it none then or afterwards. In two days more we came to an old Spanish Fort, dismantled and deserted, which had been built many years before in expectation of an invasion from the United States. This was about one hundred miles from Sante Fe. We soon encountered large herds of sheep, attended by Shepherds, and on the second day after passing the Fort, came to a small town in a narrow ravine on the Peccas river and at the foot of a high cliff. Here I became acquainted with an old Spaniard, named Ortiso, who in his youth had been captured by the Pawnees and sold to Chouteau of St. Louis, where he had learned French and whence he returned home by the way of New Orleans, St. Antoine in Texas and the interior of Mexico. He informed me more particularly than I had yet heard, of the Mexican Revolution, and foretold that Iturbide would be elected President at the ensuing election. We proceeded up the bank of the Peccas by a narrow road, impassable for waggons. One of the horses with all my powder and some of the most valuable goods, here fell down a precipice into a beaver dam in the river. The horse was uninjured but the goods were nearly all spoiled. The next town on our route was Sam Miguel, fifteen miles from the last, an old Spanish town of about a hundred houses, a large church, and two miserably constructed flour mills. Here was the best water-power for mills, and the country in the vicinity abounded in the finest pine timber I had ever seen. But no attempt is made to improve the immense advantages which nature offers. Every thing that the inhabitants were connected with seemed going to decay. We left San Miguel on the following morning with the Alcalde and a company of Spaniards bound for Sante Fe. We stopped at night at the ancient Indian village of Peccas about fifteen miles from San Miguel. I slept in the Fort, which encloses two or three acres in an oblong, the sides of which are bounded by brick houses three stories high, and without any entrances in front. The window frames were five feet long and three-fourths of a foot in width, being made thus narrow to prevent all ingress through them. The lights were made of izing-glass and each story was sup-

plied with similar windows. A balcony surmounted the
first and second stories and moveable ladders were used
in ascending to them on the front. We entered the Fort
by a gate which led into a large square. On the roofs,
which like those of all the houses in Mexico are flat,
were large heaps of stones for annoying an enemy. I
noticed that the timbers which extended out from the
walls about six feet and supported the balconies, were all
hewn with stone hatchets. The floors were of brick, laid
on poles, bark and mortar. The brick was burned in the
sun and made much larger than ours, being about two
feet by one. The walls were covered with plaster made
of lime and izing-glass. I was informed by the Spaniards
and Indians that this town and Fort are of unknown
antiquity, and stood there in considerable splendor in the
time of the Conquerors. The climate being dry and equ-
able and the wood in the buildings the best of pine and
cedar, the towns here suffer but little by natural decay.
The Indians have lost all tradition of the settlement of
the town of Peccas. It stood a remarkable proof of the
advance made by them in the arts of civilization before
the Spaniards came among them. All the houses are well
built and showed marks of comfort and refinement. The
inhabitants, who were all Indians, treated us with great
kindness and hospitality. In the evening I employed an
Indian to take my horses to pasture, and in the morning
when he brought them up I asked him what I should
pay him. He asked for powder and I was about to give
him some, when the Spanish officer forbade me, saying
it was against the law to supply the Indians with amunition. Arms are kept out of their hands by their masters
who prohibit all trade in those articles with any of the
tribes around them. On the next day in the evening, we
came in sight of Santa Fe, which presented a fine appearance in the distance. It is beautifully situated on a

plain of dry and rolling ground, at the foot of a high mountain, and a small stream which rises in the mountain to the west runs directly through the city. It contained a population at this time of six thousand. The houses were all white-washed outside and in, and presented a very neat and pleasing sight to the eye of the traveller. They are all flat on the roof and most of them one story in height. There are five very splendid churches, all Roman Catholic, which are embellished with pictures, and ornaments of gold and silver in the most costly style. The chalises were of pure gold and candlesticks of silver. The principal buildings, including the Fort, are built around the public square in the middle of the city. The Fort, which occupies the whole side of this square, encloses about ten acres, and is built on the plan of the Peccas Fort above described. There is an outer wall about eight feet in height, enclosing the buildings, which like those at Peccas bound the inner square. The whole was falling to decay and but few soldiers were stationed in it. The farms are without fences or walls, and the cattle, hogs, &c., have to be confined during the raising and harvesting of crops. They raise onions, peas, beans, corn, wheat and red pepper—the last a principal ingredient in Spanish food. Potatoes and turnips were unknown. I saw peach trees, but none of apples, cherries, or pears. The gardens were enclosed.

The country is entirely destitute of rains except in the month of June and July, when the rivers are raised to a great height. A continual drought prevails throughout all the rest of the year, not even relieved by dews. Consequently the ground has to irrigated by means of the many streams which rise in the mountains and flow into the Rio Grande; and for this purpose canals are cut through every farm. Land that can be watered is of immense value, while that which is not near the streams is worthless. While in Sante Fe, a Spaniard took me six-teen miles south, to show me his farm of 15 acres, for which he had just paid $100 per acre, and which lay conveniently to water. Hogs and poultry are scarce, while sheep, goats, and cattle are very abundant.

CHAPTER IV

Interview with Governor Malgaris—Commencement of business—Departure of McKnight—Arrival of Cordaro—His Speech—His visit to Nacotoche—His death and character—Hugh Glenn—Celebration of Mexican Independence—Gambling and dissipation—Mexican Indians—Domestic manufactures—Visit of the Utahs—Their Horses—Speech of the Chief Lechat—War with the Navahoes—Cowardly murder of their Chiefs by the Spaniards—Militia of Santa Fe—Attempt to go to Senoria—Stopped by the Governor—Interview with the Adjutant—Selling out—Hugh Glenn again—How the Governor paid me a Debt—Spanish Justice—Departure for home.

I ENTERED SANTE FE on the first day of December, A. D. 1821, and immediately went with Ortise as interpreter, to the Governor's *palatia* or house, to whom I made known my object in visiting his country, and showed my passport. He remarked on reading it, that they were entirely independent of Spain, that the new government had not laid any duties on imports and gave me permission to vend my goods. I rented a house, and on the next day commenced business. In about two weeks I took in $200, which I advanced to John McKnight for the expenses of his journey to Durango, about sixteen hundred miles south, where his brother Robert was living after his enlargement from prison. They both returned in the month of April following. Soon after McKnights departure, I heard of Hugh Glenn's arrival at Loas, sixty miles north of Santa Fe and was soon after favored with a visit from him. He came down to Santa Fe, borrowed

84

$60 from me, and at the end of a week returned to Loas.

About six weeks after I reached Santa Fe my true friend and protector, Cordaro, came in according to promise, with thirty of his tribe, to ascertain if we were at liberty. He was dressed in his full regimentals and commanded the respect of the Spanish officials, who behaved towards him with great deference. By his request a council was held, which convened in the Spanish Council House on the public square, and was attended by the Spanish officers, magistrates, and principal citizens of Santa Fe. Cordaro made the speech for which he had caused the council to be held. He expressed his pleasure at finding that we and the Spaniards were friends, that he would be pleased to see us always living together like brothers and hoped that the American trade would come to his country as well as to the Spaniards. He complained that we traded with their enemies, the Osages, and furnished them with powder, lead, and guns, but had no intercourse with the Camanches. He hoped the Government of the United States would interfere and stop the depredations of the Osages upon his nation. "They steal our horses and murder our people," said he, "and the Americans sell them the arms and amunition which they use in war upon us. We want your trade, and if you will come among us we will not cheat nor rob you. I have had a talk with my nation and told them they had done a great wrong in treating you as they did, and they promised never to do so again. They say they will pay you in horses and mules for the goods they took from you on the Canadian, if you will only come once more into our country. Come with your goods among us; you shall be well treated. I pledge you my word, the word of Cordaro, that you shall not be hurt nor your goods taken from you without full payment. Each of my nation promises to give you a horse if you will come and trade with us once more, and though poor, and though I got none of your goods, yet will I give you two of the best horses in the nation. Come to our country once more and you shall find friends among the Camanches. Come and you shall be safe. Cordaro says it." The old warrior spoke like a orator and looked like a statesman. He appeared conscious of the vast superiority of the whites, or rather of the Americans, to his own race and desired the elevation of his countrymen by adopting some of our improvements and customs. For the Spaniards he entertained a strong aversion and dislike; not at all mingled with fear, however, for he spoke to them always as an equal or superior. They refused to trade with his nation in arms and had nothing besides which his people wanted. Their remarkable disposition to treachery appeared to be perfectly known to the old Chieftain.

After the council, Cordaro desired me to write a letter for him to his great friend Col. Jameson of Nacatoche, and make known to him the manner in which he had remembered his promise to protect the Americans in his country, by saving me and my company from death at the hands of his countrymen. I wrote the letter and delivered it to him. On the next day we parted, and I never saw him again. In my trip to the Camanche country in 1824 I was informed by the Indians that he went to Nacatoche with my letter to Col. Jameson, who gave him three horses, loaded with presents. By this means he returned to his country a rich man, and soon after became sick and died. He was a sagacious, right-hearted patriot and a brave warrior, who in different circumstances might have accomplished the destiny of a hero and savior of his country.

I continued my trading, though without much success on account of the scarcity of money. I had seen enough of Mexican society to be thoroughly disgusted with it. I had not supposed it possible for any society to be as profligate and vicious as I found all ranks of that in Santa Fe. The Indians are much superior to their Spanish masters in all the qualities of a useful and meritorious population.

On the fifth of February a celebration took place of Mexican Independence. A few days before this appointed time, a meeting of the Spanish officers and principal citizens was held at the house of the Alcalde to make arrangements for the celebration. They sent for me, asked what was the custom in my country on such occasions, and requested my advice in the matter. I advised them to raise a liberty pole, hoist a flag, and fire a salute for each Province. They counted up the Provinces or States, and discovered that Mexico contained twenty-one, including Texas. They said they knew nothing of the rule of proceeding in such cases and desired me to superintend the work. I sent out men to the neighboring mountains for the tallest pine that could be found. They returned with one thirty feet long. I sent them out again, and they brought in another much longer than the first. I spliced these together, prepared a flag rope, and raised the whole, as a liberty pole, about seventy feet high. There was now great perplexity for a national emblem and motto for the flag, none having yet been devised, and those of Spain being out of the question. I recommended the Eagle, but they at last agreed upon two clasped hands in sign of brotherhood and amity with all nations. By day light on the morning of the fifth I was aroused to direct the raising of the flag. I arose and went to the square, where I found about a dozen men with the Governor, John Facundo Malgaris, all in a quandary, not knowing what to do. I informed the Governor that all was ready for raising the flag, which honor belonged to him. "Oh do it yourself," said he, "you understand such things." So,

I raised the first flag in the free and independent State of New Mexico. As the flag went up, the cannon fired and men and women from all quarters of the city came running, some half dressed, to the public square, which was soon filled with the population of this city. The people of the surrounding country also came in, and for five days the square was covered with Spaniards and Indians from every part of the province. During this whole time the city exhibited a scene of universal carousing and revelry. All classes abandoned themselves to the most reckless dissipation and profligacy. No Italian carnival ever exceeded this celebration in thoughtlessness, vice and licentiousness of every description. Men, women and children crowded every part of the city, and the carousal was kept up equally by night and day. There seemed to be no time for sleep. Tables for gambling surrounded the square and continually occupied the attention of crowds. Dice and Faro-banks were all the time in constant play. I never saw any people so infatuated with the passion for gaming. Women of rank were seen betting at the Faro-banks and dice tables. They frequently lost all their money; then followed the jewelry from their fingers, arms and ears: then the ribose or sash edged with gold, which they wear over the shoulders, was staked and lost, when the fair gamesters would go to their homes for money to redeem the last pledge and if possible, continue the play. Men and women on all sides of me, were thus engaged, and were all equally absorbed in the fluctuating fortunes of these games. The Demon of chance and of avarice seemed to possess them all, to the loss of what little reason nature had originally made theirs. One universal jubilee, like bedlam broke loose, reigned in Santa Fe for five days and nights. Freedom without restraint or license, was the order of the day; and thus did these rejoicing republicans continue the celebration of their Independence, till nature was too much exhausted to support the dissipation any longer. The crowds then dispersed to their homes with all the punishments of excess, with which pleasure visits her votaries. I saw enough during this five days revelry to convince me that the republicans of New Mexico were unfit to govern themselves or any body else. The Indians acted with more moderation and reason in their rejoicing than the Spaniards. On the second day of the celebration a large company of men and women from San Felipe, an Indian town forty miles south of Santa Fe, marched into the city, displaying the best formed persons I had yet seen in the country. The men were a head taller than the Spaniards around them, and their women were extremely beautiful, with fine figure and a graceful, elegant carriage. They were all tastefully dressed in cotton cloth of their own weaving and decorated with coral beads of a brilliant red color. Many wore rich pearl necklaces and jewelry of great value. I was told by Ortise that the ornaments of stone, silver and gold which some of these Indian ladies wore, were worth five hundred dollars. The red coral was worth one hundred dollars per pound. Many of the Indians, as the reader may suppose from this description of their women, are very wealthy. The men were also elegantly dressed in fine cloth, manufactured by their own wives and daughters. The Americans with their Tariff and "protection of home industry," might learn a lesson from these wise and industrious Indians. I heard nothing among them of a Tariff to protect their "domestic manufactures." They worked and produced and protection came of itself without the curse of government interference. This Indian company danced very gracefully upon the public square to the sound of a drum and the singing of the older members of their band. In this exercise they displayed great skill and dexterity. When intermingled in apparently hopeless confusion in a very complicated figure, so that the dance seemed on the point of breaking up, suddenly at the tap of the drum, each found his partner and each couple their place, without the least disorder and in admirable harmony. About the same time the Peccas Indians came into the city, dressed in skins of bulls and bears. At a distance their disguise was quite successful and they looked like the animals which they counterfeited so well that the people fled frightened at their appearance, in great confusion from the square.

I have spoken before, in favorable terms of the Mexican Indians. They are a nobler race of people than their masters the descendants of the conquerors; more courageous and more generous; more faithful to their word and more ingenious and intellectual than the Spaniards. The men are generally six feet in stature, well formed and of an open, frank, and manly deportment. Their women are very fascinating, and far superior in virtue, as in beauty, to the greater number of the Spanish females. I was informed that all the tribes, the Utahs, the Navahoes, and others inhabiting the country west of the Mountains to the Gulf of California, like those in Mexico, lived in comfortable houses, raised wheat and corn, and had good mills for grinding their grain. I saw many specimens of their skills in the useful arts, and brought home with me some blankets and counterpanes, of Indian manufacture, of exquisite workmanship, which I have used in my family for twenty-five years. They are, generally far in advance of the Spaniards around them, in all the arts of civilized life as well as in the virtues that give value to national character.

In the latter part of February 1 received a deputation of fifty Indians from the Utah tribe on the west side of the mountains. They came riding into the city, and paraded on the public square, all well mounted on the most elegant horses I had ever seen. The animals were of a very superior breed, with their slender tapering legs and short, fine hair, like our best blooded racers. They were of almost every color, some spotted and striped as if painted for ornament. The Indians alighted at the Council House and sent a request for me to visit them. On arriving I found them all awaiting me in the Council House, with a company of Spanish officers and gentlemen led hither by curiosity. On entering I was greeted by the Chief and his companions, who shook hands with me. The Chief, whose name was Lechat, was a young man of about thirty and of a right Princely port and bearing. He told me in the Spanish language, which he spoke fluently, that he had come expressly to see me and have a talk with me. "You are Americans, we are told, and you have come from your country afar off to trade with the Spaniards. We want your trade. Come to our country with your goods. Come and trade with the Utahs. We have horses, mules and sheep, more than we want. We heard that you wanted beaver skins. The beavers in our country are eating up our corn. All our rivers are full of them. Their dams back up the water in the rivers all along their course from the mountains to the Big water. Come over among us and you shall have as many beaver skins as you want." Turning round and pointing to the Spaniards, in most contemptuous manner and with a scornful look he said, "What can you get from these? They have nothing to trade with you. They have nothing but a few poor horses and mules, a little puncha, and a little tola (tobacco and corn meal porridge) not fit for any body to use. They are poor—too poor for you to trade with. Come among the Utahs if you wish to trade with profit. Look at our horses here. Have the Spaniards any such horses? No, they are too poor. Such as these we have in our country by the thousand, and also cattle, sheep and mules. These Spaniards," said he, turning and pointing his finger at them in a style of contempt which John Randolph would have envied, "what are they? What have they? They wont even give us two loads of powder and lead for a beaver skin, and for a good reason they have not as much as they want themselves. They have nothing that you want. We have every thing that they have, and many things that they have not." Here a Spaniard cried out: "You have no money." Like a true stump orator the Utah replied, "and you have very little. You are *depicca*." In other words you are poor miserable devils and we are the true capitalists of the country. With this and much more of the same purport, he concluded his harangue, which was delivered in the most independent and lordly manner possible. He looked like a King upbraiding his subjects for being poor, when they might be rich, and his whole conduct seemed to me like bearding a wild beast in his den. The "talk" being had, Lechat produced the *calama* or pipe, and we smoked together in the manner of the Indians. I sent to my store and procured six plugs of tobacco and some handkerchiefs, which I presented to him and his company, telling them when they smoked the tobacco with their Chiefs to remember the Americans, and treat all who visited their country from mine as they would their own brothers. The council now broke up and the Chief, reiterating his invitations to me to visit his country, mounted his noble steed, and with his company rode out of the city, singing and displaying the handkerchiefs I had presented them, from the ends of their lances as standards. They departed without the least show of respect for the Spaniards, but rather with a strong demonstration on the part of Lechat of contempt for them. I noticed them at the council enquiring of this Chief with considerable interest what the

Navahoes were doing, and whether they were preparing
to attack the Spanish settlements. They had been at war
with this tribe for several years, and seemed to fear that
the Utahs might take part in it as allies of the Navahoes,
for which reason they conducted themselves with the utmost respect and forbearance towards Lechat and his
band. What was the immediate cause of this war, I did
not learn, but I saw and heard enough of it to enlist my
sympathies with the Navahoes. A few days after the visit
of the Utahs, I saw a solitary Indian of that tribe, crossing the public square in the direction of the Governor's
house, and driving before him a fat heifer. He went up to
the Governor's door, to whom he sent word that he had
a present for him, and was admitted. What followed I
learned from Ortise, an old Alcalde, with whom I boarded
during the time of my stay in Santa Fe. As he entered the
room of the Governor, the Navaho prostrated himself on
his face. The Governor stepped towards him and with a
spurning motion of the foot, which touched the Indians
head, asked him who he was and what he wanted. The
poor Indian arose on his knees and said he was a Navaho,
and had come to implore peace for his nation. "We are
tired of war and we want peace," said he; "our crops
are destroyed, our women and children are starving. Oh!
give us peace!" The Governor asked the interpreter what
he said, and being told, the *christian* replied—"Tell him
I do not want peace, I want war." With this answer the
Indian was dismissed, the Governor keeping his heifer.
The poor fellow came to my store, announced his name
and nation, and requested me to go among his tribe and
trade. He said the rivers were full of beaver and beaver
dams—that they had horses and mules which they would
exchange for powder, lead and tobacco. The Indians are
destitute of amunition and guns, and Spanish laws prohibit all trade with them in these articles. I gave him

several plugs of tobacco, a knife and other small articles, and told him when he went back to his country to smoke my tobacco with his Chiefs and tell them if any Americans came to their country to treat them like brothers. He went off with a guard as far as the outposts on the route to his country. But I have no doubt he was murdered by the Spaniards long before reaching his home. About a week after this, sixteen Navaho Chiefs came into the town of St. James, sixty miles below Santa Fe on the Del Norte, and requested the commander of the Fort to allow them to pass on to the Governor at Santa Fe, saying that they had come to make peace. The commander invited them into the Fort, smoked with them and made a show of friendship. He had placed a Spaniard on each side of every Indian as they sat and smoked in a circle, and at a signal each Indian was seized by his two Spanish companions and held fast while others despatched them by stabbing each one to the heart. A Spaniard who figured in this butchery showed me his knife which he said had killed eight of them. Their dead bodies were thrown over the wall of the Fort and covered with a little earth in a gully. A few days afterwards five more of the same nation appeared on the bank of the river opposite the town, and enquired for their countrymen. The Spaniards told them they had gone on to Sante Fe, invited them to come over the river, and said they should be well treated. They crossed and were murdered in the same manner as the others. There again appeared three Indians on the opposite bank, enquiring for their Chiefs. They were decoyed across, taken into the town under the mask of friendship, and also murdered in cold blood. In a few days two more appeared, but could not be induced to cross; when some Spanish horsemen went down the river to intercept them. Perceiving this movement, they fled and no more embassies

came in. The next news that came told of a descent made
by the Navahoes in great force, on the settlements in
the south, in which they killed all of every age and condition, burned and destroyed all they could not take
away with them, and drove away the sheep, cattle and
horses. They came from the south directly towards Santa
Fe, sweeping everything before them, and leaving the
land desolate behind them. They recrossed the Del Norte
below Santa Fe, and passed to the north, laid bare the
country around the town of Toas, and then disappeared
with all their booty. While this was going on, Malgaris
was getting out the militia, and putting nearly all the
inhabitants under arms, preparatory to an expedition. I
was requested to go, but I preferred to be a spectator in
such a war. The militia of Santa Fe when on parade,
beggared all description. Falstaff's company was well
equipped and well furnished compared with these troops
of Gov. Malgaris! Such a gang of tatterdemallions I never
saw before or since. They were of all colors, with all
kinds of dresses and every species of arms. Some were
bare headed, others bare backed—some had hats without
rims or crowns, and some wore coats without skirts;
others again wore coats without sleeves. Most of them
were armed with bows and arrows. A few had guns that
looked as if they had been imported by Cortez, while
others had iron hoops fastened to the ends of poles,
which passed for lances. The doughty Governor Facunda
Malgaris, on foot, in his cloak and chapeau de bras, was
reviewing this noble army. He was five feet high, nearly
as thick as he was long, and as he waddled from one end
of the line to the other I thought of Alexander and Han-
nibal and Caesar, and how their glories would soon be
eclipsed by this hero of Santa Fe. After him followed the
Adjutant in his jacket with red cuffs and collar, and
with his frog-sticker, called a sword, at his side. He

examined the bows and arrows, lances and other arms of
these invincibles. He with the little Governor seemed big
with the fate of New Mexico. At last when all was ready
the Governor sent them forth to the war and himself
went to his dinner. In the mean time where was the
enemy—the blood-thirsty Navahoes? They had returned
in safety to their own country with all their plunder, and
were even then far beyond the reach of Gov. Malgaris'
troop of scare crows.

In the beginning of March finding that trade was dull
and money very scarce in Santa Fe, I enquired for a
better place of business and was advised by Ortise to go
to Senora on the Gulf of California, where gold and
silver was more abundant than in New Mexico. I requested him to go with me; he declined going himself
but procured his brother, whom I hired, to go as guide
for $12, for each mule load. I packed up my goods, and
had got ready for the journey when Ortise came in with
a gloomy countenance and asked if I had asked permission of the Governor to go to Senora. I said I had not,
and he advised me to see him. I went to his house, ap-
prehensive of hostility, and found the dignitary walking
with a lordly air up and down his piazza. As I approached
he strutted away from me to the opposite end of the
gallery without deigning to notice me. I stood and awaited
his return, and as he came up, I accosted him politely,
and said I could not sell my goods in Santa Fe and had
called to obtain his permission to go with them to Senora,
where I had understood money was more plenty than
in Santa Fe. "You can't go sir," growled his Excellency,
and continued his promenade. I followed and asked him
why I could not go. He said he had no orders to let me
go. I asked him if he had any orders to prevent me. He
said no. I then said, you know that I have a passport from
my government, approved by the Spanish minister. "Oh

we have nothing to do with the Spanish Government."
But you have something to do with my Government. I
shall start for Senora, and if you arrest or imprison me
on my way, my Government shall hear from me. This appeared to agitate the little grandee and set him to think-
ing for a moment. He paced to and fro a while, stopped
short, and asked how I was going. With Don Francisco
Ortise, as guide. At this he burst into a loud laugh. "Ho,
ho! Don Francisco will go with you, will he? Well Don
Thomas, you can go, but I will send a party of soldiers
with you to the outposts, and if any Spaniard attempt to
go further with you I will have him brought back in
irons and thrown into prison. You will have to pass
through the country of the Apaches, and you will be
robbed, perhaps murdered if you have no Spaniard with
you. Now go, Don Thomas, now go—ha, ha, ha." I now
'turned and left him. Ortise, whom I considered my
friend, advised me by no means, to make the attempt
to reach Senora without a Spanish guide and I gave up
the project. I regarded this, the result of a plot to detain
me in Santa Fe till Spring, when they knew I was to
return, and would have to sell my goods at any price. I
went on the evening of my interview with the Governor,
to the house of a sick Lieutenant, where I found the
Adjutant and several other officers. They asked, with a
sly glance at each other, when I was going to Senora. I
am not going. "Why so, we heard you were all ready to
start. You have a passport, have you not?" Yes, said I, but
the Governor threatens to imprison any Spaniard that attempts to go with me. He has imprisoned all my countrymen that came here before me, and I suppose, if he dared,
he would imprison me. Here the sick Lieutenant shook
my knee by way of caution, and the Adjutant leaped up
exclaiming, "If he dared! What do you mean sir, be careful how you talk;" and put his hand on the butcher knife

at his side, called a sword. I had a dirk at my breast, as good a weapon as his, and facing him I repeated, yes, if he dared; but he dares not, nor dare any of you imprison me while I observe your laws. You have robbed and imprisoned all my countrymen heretofore, but my Government will now stop this baseness and cruelty to the Americans. If you violate my rights while I have an American passport my Government will avenge my wrongs on your heads. This appeared to cool the Adjutant, who said we were friends and that he would not tell the Governor. Tell him or not as you please said I.

I wish for the honor of my country, or rather of my Government, that the name of American citizen were a better protection in a foreign country than it is. Ancient Rome and modern England are examples to us in this respect. A subject of the English monarchy in a foreign country is sure that any flagrant violation of his natural rights will be avenged, if necessary, by the whole military and naval power of his country. An Englishman like an ancient Roman citizen, knows that his Government will look after him and is sure of protection. An American is sure of nothing. His Government may amid the turmoil of electioneering, demand him from his jailors, but it is much more likely to overlook him entirely as beneath its regard. The case of Robert McKnight, who returned in April with John, his brother, from Durango, after an imprisonment of ten years, was a remarkable instance of the delinquency of our Government in this particular. His goods had been confiscated and himself and his companions thrown into prison, where they remained ten years, and during the whole time their own Government was sleeping on their wrongs. No notice whatever was taken of them; and when McKnight returned to his country he was equally unsuccessful in seeking redress. "I will go back to Mexico, said he, swear allegiance to their Gov-

ernment and become a citizen. I have resided the pre-
scribed term of years, and there is a better chance for
obtaining justice from the Mexicans, scoundrels as they
are, than from my own Government. I will go and recover
as a citizen of Mexico what I lost as a citizen of the
United States. My own Government refuses to do me
justice, and I will renounce it forever. I would not raise
a straw in its defence." He accordingly returned to Mexico, where he probably received remuneration for his
losses, and where he now lives a citizen of the country.

While in Santa Fe I was a frequent visitor at the house
of the parish Priest, a very gentlemanly, intelligent man,
where I often found an interesting company assembled. I
supped at his house on one occasion with sixteen Spanish gentlemen of education, and some of distinction. The
conversation happened to turn on the power and condition of the United States, and particularly on the country west of the Mississippi. They said the country west
of this river once belonged to them, and agreed that it
would some day return to their possession. They said
that Spain had ceded it to Bonaparte without their con-
sent, and that, it of right, belonged to Mexico. They also
expressed great dissatisfaction with the line of the Sabine,
alleging that it ought to have been and would yet be
the Mississippi instead of the former river. I told them
that my countrymen were also dissatisfied with the Sabine as the boundary. "Ah exclaimed one, then we shall
have little difficulty in changing it; both sides will be
agreed." Not so fast, said I, we think the boundary ought
to have been the Rio Del Norte. "What! said they, the
Del Norte; that would take in Santa Fe." Yes, Seignors,
said I, we claim to the Del Norte. "Never, never—you will
never get it, and if it ever comes to a trial of power between Mexico and the States, we will have to the Mississippi. You will be compelled to give it to us." I told them

to mark my words and said, if ever the boundary is changed you will see it go westward and not to the east.

The Spring was nearly gone and most of my goods remained unsold. Money was very scarce, and I had little prospect of selling them at any price. I offered them at cost, and at last found a purchaser of most of them in a Spaniard named Pino, who paid me one thousand dollars in cash and an equal sum in horses and mules. He borrowed the money of Francisco Chavis, the father of Antonio, who was murdered in the United States by Mason, Brown and McDaniel. The last two were convicted of the murder on the testimony of Mason, and executed in St. Louis in 1844. After this trade with Pino I had still on my hands a large quantity of brown and grey cloths, which were unsaleable in the Spanish market; blue and other colors being preferred. These cloths I sold to Hugh Glenn, who again honored me with a visit in the latter part of May, staid with me two weeks, borrowed forty dollars, in addition to the sixty I had already loaned him, and gave me his note for the money and goods, which (the note) I have held to this day. He wanted the goods to sell to his company who were trapping near Toas, and promised to pay me the money as soon as he reached St. Louis and disposed of his beaver fur. Taking him for a man of honor I treated him as such, to my own loss. I was now ready to depart for home, having disposed or got rid rather of my goods and collected all my debts except one from the Governor. During the winter his Excellency had sent his Excellency's Secretary to my store for some samples of cloth. The Secretary after taking these with some shawls for the examination of his master, returned and purchased goods for his Excellency to the sum of eighty-three dollars and told me to charge them to his Excellency. I did so, and on the day before my departure I called at his Excel-

lency's house and found his Excellency looking every
inch a Governor, and very pompously pacing the piazza
as was the custom of his Excellency. I remarked that I
was going home. "Very well," said his Excellency, "you
can go;" and walked on. I awaited his Excellency's return, and again remarked that I was going home; that I
did not expect to return, and would be thankful for
the amount of his Excellency's account with me. "I have
not a dollar. The Government has not paid me in ten
years, and how can I pay my creditors." I offered to take
two mules. "I have no more mules than I want myself,"
said his Excellency. With this I parted forever with Gov.
Malgaris of New Mexico. Ortise told me I could not
sue him as he was "the head of the law."

Some time before this I saw a Spaniard who had been
imprisoned for more than a year, and was then set at
liberty. He had just come from the Commandant, whom
he asked for the cause of his imprisonment. "You are at
liberty now, are you not?" "Yes; but I wish to know why
I have been so long deprived of liberty." "You are at liberty now, and that is enough for you to know," said the
Commandant: And this was all the satisfaction the poor
Spaniard could get. The following will illustrate the sum-
mary method of administering justice in Santa Fe. There
were many American deserters in the city from the
Fort at Nacatoche, some of whom had lived here sixteen
years, and were generally of bad character. Robert Mc-
Knight had entrusted one of these, named Finch, with a
valuable sword to sell for him. Finch pawned the sword
for twelve dollars, and seeing him with money I told
McKnight he would never get any thing for his sword as
Finch was spending the money he had raised on it. "There
is no danger," said he, "Finch would not trifle with me."
On the next day he demanded his sword or the money
from Finch, who refused to give him any satisfaction;

whereupon McKnight seized and dashed him about twelve feet, head foremost against a door of the Fort. I interfered and saved Finch from any further injury than a severe cut on his head. He then confessed the fact of his having pawned the sword and named the place where it could be found. McKnight now went before the Alcalde, a stern old Spaniard, who called his officer and handed him his gold headed cane as a warrant bringing up Finch, the sword and the pawnee. They all arrived, Finch with his head tied up in a handkerchief, when the Alcade took the sword from the Spaniard who had taken it in pledge, and asked him if he knew for what purpose Finch had received it. He admitted that Finch told him at the time of pawning it, that he had received it to sell. "Then," said the Alcalde, "if you had bought it, though only for five dollars, you could now keep it, but you had no right to take it in pawn;" and thereupon handed the sword to McKnight as the true owner. "But who will pay me my twelve dollars?" said the bailee. "That lies between you and Finch." "And what am I to get for my broken head," said Finch. "I know nothing about that Finch," said the magistrate, "but if you do not behave yourself better than you have done of late, I will drive you out of the province." So, McKnight got his sword and a little revenge without having a bill of costs or lawyer's fee to pay.

Most of my company had been engaged in trapping during my stay in Santa Fe, and some had gone far into the interior of Mexico. Collecting such as remained, and in company with the McKnights, I now, on the first of June 1822, bade adieu forever to the capital of New Mexico, and was perfectly content never to repeat my visit to it or any other part of the country.

CHAPTER V

Col. Glenn's conversion—His profits thereby—Avenues to New Mexico—An instance of Spanish treachery and cruelty—Glenn's cowardice—Meeting with the Pawnees—Mexican Indians—Battle between the Pawnees and Osages—Disappearance of Glenn—Chouteau and the Osages—Indian revenge—Passage of the Shoshoua—Singular Ferrying—Entrance into Missouri—Robbery by the Osages—Interview with Missionaries—Arrival at St. Louis—More of Glenn—Home—Still greater troubles with creditors than with the Indians.

I STARTED FROM Santa Fe with Hugh Glenn on his return to Toas, whence he was to go with me to St. Louis. On arriving at the Spanish village of San Domingo, about thirty miles north of Santa Fe and five from the Indian village of St. John, we stopped by invitation, at the house of the parish Priest, where the principal citizens visited us during the evening. Here I was somewhat astonished to hear Glenn, late at night, tell the Priest that he wished to be baptised and join the Church. He said in answer to the Priest's questions, that he had entertained this intention for a long time before coming to this country; that he had endeavored to instruct himself in relation to the tenets of the Church, and produced a Catholic book, called the "Pious Guide." The Priest told him to reflect on the subject and pray to the Almighty for light. In the morning Glenn appeared with a very sanctimonious face, and repeated his request. The Priest questioned him on the Catholic faith and the noviciate answered very

103

intelligently. It being Sunday, they went to the Church to have the ceremony of baptism performed on the new convert. Leroy, one of his company, acted as God-father, and the Priest procured a very respectable old lady of the place to act as God-mother. The saintly Colonel Glenn looked the very picture of sanctity during the performance of the rite; and he afterwards made a good penny by the operation. The people were very fond of their new convert, and showered honors and presents on Col. Glenn. He was talking of coming back from the States with goods for this market, and many of the inhabitants entrusted him with mules and money to make purchases for them, of which they never heard again. Among his religious rewards was a lot of the finest Indian blankets. The Colonel was a great and good man among the people from this time and bore the cross of his religion with edifying humility.

On the next day we reached Toas, a small settlement near the mountains, in a beautiful and fertile valley through which the Rio Grande flows and offers most valuable inducements ·to the manufacturer by its water power; but none are here found with sufficient enterprise to seize the offer. The country in the hands of the Americans would bloom like a garden, while now it languishes in a state of half wilderness—half cultivation.

Leaving Toas with eighty-three horses and mules, with Glenn and his company who had about sixty, we travelled in one day half way over the mountains, stopping at night in the middle of the pass. Here we were overtaken by some Spaniards with a mule load of bread, biscuit, sugar, chocolate and other delicacies, all sent as a present to the godly Glenn by his God-mother. He took them, I suppose, with pious thankfulness, much as a hog takes the acorns that fall to him from an oak tree—without ever looking up. On my return to St. Louis I heard of Glenn's sneers and ridicule of the clergy of New Mexico. The truth concerning them was bad enough, but I was astonished to hear them villified and abused by the so lately converted Col. Glenn. He changed his religion more rapidly than his clothes, and made each change a profitable speculation to himself. Such pliability of conscience may serve a temporary purpose to its fortunate possessor, but I have found very few of my countrymen, thank God, so base as to practise hypocrisy to the alarming extent to which this sordid miscreant carried its exercise.

On the next day we marched to the foot of the mountain over which we had travelled for about fifty miles, with the utmost ease through a regular and even pass with a very gradual ascent half the distance and thence with an equally gradual descent. There are three principal routes over the mountains to New Mexico. One below San Miguel, by which I went to Santa Fe, and which is easily passible for a large army without danger of surprise. The second, through which I was now returning to the States, and the third, a few miles to the north of this last and of Toas, are both excellent passes for travellers and emigrants, but would not admit of an army in the face of an enemy. They are quite narrow and closed in by mountains of a great height and by numerous defiles, which in possession of an enemy would present great obstacles to an invading army. McKnight, who came through the northern pass, informed me that it was much better than this, near Toas. These three passes are all of slight elevation, and present a gradual ascent and descent for about fifty miles, of no difficulty to the passenger and his teams. The most northern pass will probably become the great outlet of American emigration to California.

At the end of our two days journey from Toas we en-

camped at the foot of the mountain near large piles of
stones placed on each side of a ravine or gully. These
were in shape like immense walls, from ten to sixty feet
in length, about ten wide, and from four to six feet in
height. They were the tombs of Camanche Indians, who
had been massacred at this place many years before by
the Spaniards. An old man in Santa Fe whom I employed
about my store, informed me of the circumstances of this
cold blooded butchery, in which he as a Spanish soldier
took part. It happened when my informant was about
twenty years of age, which was a few years previous to
our revolutionary war. According to his account, the
Spaniards and Camanches had been at war with each
other for many years with various fortune on both sides,
when the Spanish authorities determined to offer peace
to their enemies. For this purpose they marched with a
large army to this place of tombs, and encamped, whence
they sent out heralds to the Camanches with an invitation
to the whole nation to come in and smoke the pipe of
peace and bury the hatchet of war forever. The un-
suspecting Indians came in pursuant to the invitation,
and brought their women and children to the number
of several thousands. The council was held and a solemn
treaty formed which one side hoped and expected would
be inviolate forever. They smoked the pipe of peace and
of brotherhood. Every thing betokened lasting harmony,
and for three days an apparently friendly and cordial intercourse took place between the two powers. During
this time the Spaniards insidiously bought up all the bows
and arrows, and other arms of the Indians, at very high
prices, and the third day found these simple children of
nature stripped of their arms and entirely defenceless,
in the midst of their treacherous enemies. Then ensued a
scene of murder exceeding in atrocity even the celebrated
slaughter of Glenco, which occurred in Scotland a few

years before this, and under very similar circumstances. The Spaniards having surrounded the Indians, fell suddenly, at a concerted signal upon them and killed all without regard to age or sex. The women and children clung to their protectors, who would not leave them and could not fight, and thus they were all slaughtered together. The bloody work continued most of the day and the dead were left in large heaps over the ground. The drain or gully, between the stone walls ran with blood on this terrible day, as the old Spaniard told me, like a spring freshet. Not a man, woman or child was spared; and my informant supposed that the example had deterred all the tribes of Camanches from making war on the people of Santa Fe from that day to this. The citizens of this town may have been exempt from attack, but we have always heard of the incursions of these tribes on the Spanish settlements, and conduct like this of the Spaniards near Toas would, and did sow deep the seeds of incurable hate which have frequently germinated since in bloody retributions. The countrymen of the slaughtered Indians afterwards erected the stone walls near to which we were now encamped, and which covered a large extent of ground, as tombs and monuments for the dead. Their power was greatly broken by the loss of so many warriors and the nation was a long time in recovering its former strength.

On the next morning after crossing the mountain we entered the prairies, which were frequently quite broken and uneven. The spurs of the mountains were covered with pine and cedar. Directing our course to the northeast, in four days we struck the Arkansas a considerable distance from its head. On the next day, and the seventh since leaving Toas, Col. Glenn, who marched in advance of me, sent back a man with the news that the "Camanches were ahead." I hastened forward with the Mc-

Knights, and found Glenn stretched out on his blanket in a cold sweat and shaking with fear as if he had the ague. I asked, where are the Indians? "Oh there they are, hid behind that willow bar." I searched and found nothing, when Glenn again cried out, "Oh there they are," pointing to two men riding towards us on the opposite or north side of river, and also to a company of about two lodges, or twelve Indians going from us to the north-west. I soon perceived that the two men first seen were white, and one crossed the river to our company. They were a company of about twelve from Boone's Lick, of whom one was named Cooper, on their way to Santa Fe. Glenn, as much frightened as before, now insisted that the Indians whom we had seen had gone off to bring up their companions to attack us in the night. He had his horses and mules tied together and ordered his company to prepare for action. I determined to allow my horses to separate for grazing, and in looking for a good place for herding them, I espied and shot a buffalo under the cliff. This brought up all my company and a part of Glenn's to ascertain the cause of the shot, while Glenn was crying out to them, "Come back, you'll all be killed by the Indians." When I returned to the camp I told him to send some of his men for a part of the buffalo, if he wanted any meat. "No, I want no meat and I will not travel with men so rash as to fire their guns while so near the Indians." In the morning we took up our march, with one of Cooper's party on his return St. Louis, and with Glenn in advance, who, intent on getting out of danger, soon outtravelled us. About two o'clock one of his men returned at full speed, calling to us to hurry on— "here are two thousand Pawnees." On overtaking Glenn I found two Indians, who said the main army would soon be with them. I had brought with me from Toas two Mexican Indians who wished to go to the United States.

Glenn knowing that the Pawnees were at war with the Spaniards, said these Mexicans would be killed on the coming up of the Pawnee army, and implored us to let them be killed "peaceably" and not endanger the whole party by any unnecessary resistance. I replied that these Indians were under my protection and should not be hurt. In a short time we saw the whole army pouring over the bend or knowe before us, which for half a mile was red with them, all afoot, except three, and every man carrying a rope *lasso* or *cabras* in his hand. Again did Glenn shake as with the ague, and the cold sweat stood on his face in drops. "Oh they are coming, they are coming," said he. One of their three horsemen rode past our band, then returned and halted at some distance as for a parley. I told Glenn to get up from the ground where he was lying and go out to speak with this Indian. No, no, said he, we shall be shot down if we go out there. The creature's courage and senses seemed to have left him together. I went out with McKnight, shook hands with the Chiefs and brought them in among our men who spread buffalo skins on the ground for their reception, while I prepared the pipe which we smoked together. The leader of this army was a brother of the head Chief of the Pawnee nation, and one of the finest formed and best looking men I have ever seen. He was six feet in height, with large and powerful limbs, a large head, with a well developed front, and keen dark hazel eyes. His manner was dignified and commanding, and he evidently possessed the confidence of his tribe. There was something in him that at once drew out my heart towards him and secured my esteem and respect. He was now going, he told me, down to the country of the Camanches, Arrippahoes and other tribes, near the Salt Plains, to conclude treaties of peace. They had been out ten days from their country and would have passed this place five days before had not this Chief been taken sick. He now looked feverish and weak. After smoking, the whole party of Indians, to the number of one thousand, gathered around us and four of them marched my Mexican friends into the circle and placed them before the Chief above mentioned, who was sitting on the ground. All the Indians except this Chief declared that these two were Mexicans and therefore their enemies, and many called for their scalps. A Kioway Chief made a violent speech against them. He understanding the Spanish language, desired them to speak with each other. They remained silent, he then requested me to make them speak. I appeared not to understand, but said they were my men and under my protection. The Kioway then walked close to the Mexicans and in a friendly manner and confidential tone he said: "You are Spanish Indians, are you not? You can tell me; I am your friend. You know I am a Kioway; we are not at war with you. We are friends. You *are* a Spanish Indian are you not? The Mexicans looked like condemned criminals during this shower of questions, and one of them looking up and meeting the eye of the Kioway, slighly nodded an affirmative to the last question. Instantly that Chief clapped his hands and exclaimed: "Do you hear that, they acknowledge it—they are Spaniards, these are the men who have been murdering your women and children; kill them—kill them." I placed myself before the Mexicans to defend them, and told the Pawnee Chiefs they should not be killed, and the older Chiefs cried out, "come, come, go and get some wood and make fires. Kill some buffalos and get something to eat." This entirely changed the current. Loosing sight of their Mexican enemies, they ran off with a shout in obedience to their Chief and scattered over the prairies on my horses which I loaned them. Away they went in all directions and soon returned with an abundance of buffalo meat.

When they had disappeared, the Chief who had so soon dispersed them looked at me with a smile and said, pointing to the two Mexicans, "they are Spanish Indians I know; but they are with you and shall not be hurt. Last winter my brother went to Washington and saw our Great Father there. He said a great many things to my brother and made him a great many presents. And what he said went into his ear, and my brother told it again to me and it went into my ear and down to my heart. Our Great Father told my brother to treat all Americans well who visited his country, and my brother promised the Great Father, in the name of the whole nation, that we would do as he wished us to do towards the Americans. You and your friends are safe. You shall not be hurt." This Chief told me of some of his exploits as a warrior, one of which, then the latest, I will relate. His nation were at war with the Osages and in the fall before he had approached near to one of their largest villages with a war party, too small however, to risk an attack. He concealed himself and his men behind a large mound in the prairie at some distance from the village, and sent forward eight well mounted Pawnees to reconnoitre. A large party of Osages gave chase to these eight, who retreated before them to the mound and then separated, four going to the right and four to the left around the mound, and were followed by their enemies who rushed blindly into the ambuscade. Our hero, the Pawnee, now gave the war whoop, and fell upon the Osages, whose jaded horses were unable to carry them out of danger. A hundred of the Osages were killed in the fight or rather flight, and our hero, the Pawnee Chief, felt all the pride and pleasure of a Spartan in relating the triumph of his craft and valor.

We encamped at night in company with the Indians, the Chief lying near me, and in the morning nothing had been disturbed. I made presents of tobacco to the Indians and selecting one of my best horses and a Spanish saddle, bridle and rope, and leading him up to the Chief, who had no horse of his own, I presented him with this one and the trappings. The Chief appeared ashamed at not having any thing to give in return, and said, "if you ever come again to my country, I will have two horses ready for you." I told him to treat all Americans well when visiting his country, and to protect them from their enemies. He appeared greatly affected and at parting, embraced me with both arms.

After proceeding about a mile on our way we saw about thirty Indians running towards us and Glenn took another fright, said that these were coming to kill the two Mexicans, and again prayed me to give them up "peaceably." I said no, and the McKnights swore they would die themselves, rather than desert any of their comrades. They, with the rest of my company formed a circle around the Mexicans, while Glenn and his men hurried forward, and I stopped to speak with the advancing Indians. These were a hunting party belonging to the Pawnee army, who had not seen us before, having just returned from hunting, and now came to shake hands with us. They overtook Glenn for the same friendly purpose and then returned in high spirits to their countrymen. Glenn now pushed on in a trot and soon went out of my sight where he has remained from that day to this. He sold his fur in St. Louis, went to Cincinnati, and cheated me out of his debt to me, as I ought to have expected him to do after his previous cowardice and hypocricy.

We now kept our course down the Arkansas, and on the next day crossed to the north bank of the river. One of my trunks fell into the river in crossing, and some rhubarb dissolving, became mixed with my shirts, journal, invoice and other papers in the trunk, and entirely destroyed them. The writing was obliterated from the papers, and my journal which I had kept since leaving home was rendered useless. My memory, which was always very retentive of events and incidents, enables me to supply this loss with sufficient accuracy.

On the third day after parting with the Pawnees we found the prairie strewed with buffalo skeletons, and saw at a distance in a bend of the river, a company of men wearing hats. I learned afterwards that this was a company of traders bound for Santa Fe, who had been robbed by the Osages. Supposing it to be Glenn's company, I passed on without hailing them, and encamped at night in a small grove in the edge of the prairie. We secured the horses and prepared our camp with care against an attack from Indians, who were evidently in our vicinity. One-half of our band slept while the rest stood as sentinels. In the morning about an hour before day a sound of violent crying and lamentation was heard, such as is customary with the Indians when bewailing the loss of a near relation. This is usually continued from early dawn till sun-rise, when they end in a sobbing hiccough like that of children after long crying. A mounted Indian soon after day light, circled around the camp and stopped at a distance of a quarter of a mile. I cried out Mawhatonga, (long knife). The Indian repeated the word interrogatively, *Mawhatonga?* The Indians call the whites Longknives, from their swords. On my answering *howai*, (yes) this Indian came into our camp and informed me that an Osage village was near by, and that Chouteau, Tonish and Pelche, French traders, were with them. I started with the Indian for the village and came in view of it on ascending a hill a short way from the camp, where my companion went off at full speed, shouting at the top of his voice, and soon brought out the whole village with Chouteau and other French traders to meet me. A large company of Indians passed me to meet the company with the horses behind, and by their shouts and tumultuous riding gave my drove a *stampede* which made the earth shake beneath them. Chouteau invited me to breakfast with him, assuring me that my horses, which were now out of sight, would be recovered. I partook with him of a dish of coffee, the first I had tasted in twelve months, and of bread and other luxuries of civilization, which brought before my mind all the comforts of home to which I had been so long a stranger. After returning from Chouteau's *marqui,* about noon, we discovered that four horses and several articles belonging to me and McKnight and a keg of Chouteau's powder had been stolen by the Indians. Chouteau raged and stormed like a mad man and threatened to abandon the nation forever and stop all the American trade with them, unless they produced the stolen articles and abstained from molesting the property of his friends. At last two of the horses were brought up. Chouteau commanded them to return the rest of the missing goods, which however, could not be found. The Conjuror now appeared with his wand lined with bells, which he carried jingling through the village. When he started, Chouteau remarked that the lost goods would certainly be found by him; as the Indians had no hope of concealing any thing from their medicine man. The wand carried him directly towards the place of concealment, and the thieves to avoid detection soon brought up the goods which they had fortunately found. Two of my horses were lost beyond recovery. I remained with Chouteau that day till evening, and was treated by him and his French companions, like a brother. I saw a singular instance of Indian revenge, while here, which will illustrate their stern and inflexible sense of wrong. An old Osage was sitting on the ground when a younger Indian with a rope in hand stopped before him and said: "You struck

me one blow when I was a boy, I will now return it."
The sitting Indian without a murmur bent his head and
body forward to receive the justice which awaited him,
while the avenger of youthful wrongs drew two large
knots in his rope, and after swinging it around his head
several times, brought it down with all his weight upon
the back of his old enemy. The knots seemed to sink into
his back their whole depth. Leaping up in a furious rage,
the culprit rushed at the executioner, seized the rope and
endeavored to wrest it from him, claiming one blow in
return. As the pain subsided they became friends and
thought no more of the old feud. "An eye for eye and a
tooth for a tooth," is strictly their motto. The blow which
he had received when a boy, had rankled in this Indian's
heart for ten or twenty years, and now having paid it
back with interest, he was satisfied and happy. Their
method of curing diseases is very similar to the operations
of our animal magnetizers. The Conjour or Medicine man
has an old cloth, which they supposed possessed the
charm and power to restore health. With this majic cloth
assisted by other Indians in the same exercise, he rubs
the patient from head to foot, in manner similar to the
passes of the magnetizers, on their subjects. This is continued until the patient acknowledges himself relieved, or
relief is proved to be hopeless.

My company started forward before me, and I remained behind till evening with Cunigam, for the purpose of finding the two missing horses, which were
among the best. Failing in this, I with my companion, followed in the track of the company. Before we had gone
far a black cloud gathered over our heads, with thunder
and lightning in terrific grandeur. We hastened forward
till night, when the storm broke upon us in torrents of
rain which deluged the earth. We lay in the rain all night,
and in the morning the river had risen above the banks,

and nearly reached our place of sleeping. The marks of
the muddy water and leaves was visible in a straight line
on my companion as he lay asleep in a gully which the
flood had washed without waking him. We saw, a little
distance off, our company, encamped on the spot occupied by the Osages, the night but one before. Pursuing
our course down the river, we came to the Little Arkansas, which enters the main river from the north, and
crossing it, we encamped on its bank which is here very
high. The river rose twenty feet during the night from
the heavy rains which had just fallen. Here we left the
Arkansas, which goes to the south, after making what is
called the great northern bend. We travelled to the north-
east, the rain falling abundantly, and came to a creek
we were unable to cross. We encamped on its bank for
that night, and the next morning before starting, some
thirty Osages came up with some goods which they had
stolen from a party of Santa Fe traders on the Arkansas
above, and offered to us for sale. Our refusal to buy in-
censed them greatly, and they blustered and bullied
around us until we showed them plainly how little we
were effected by their bravado. One seized a belt of
McKnight's, who wrenched it out of his hands and struck
him with it a tremendous blow over the shoulder. After
these Indians left us, we pursued our course on the trail
of the Osages. The streams were all full and difficult in
crossing, and the game exceedingly scarce. In ten or
twelve days, after severe suffering for want of food, we
reached the Shoshona or Grand River, where we found
corn growing: this was just in the silk without any grain
on the ear. We boiled and ate the cob with a hearty rel-
ish. Soon after this we were hailed by Indians, who came
from the north, and finding we were whites, approached
us in a friendly manner and invited us to their village, two
miles distant. They laughed at our last meal and promised

us something better than corn cobs. We fared well, with them, on hominy, meat and bread, which last was made of flour furnished to them by Mr. Sibley, the factor at Fiery-Prairie Fort. After smoking with these friendly Osages, we proceeded on our way, and with great difficulty crossed the Shoshona, which flowed with the rapidity of a mill race. I hired some Indians to swim our horses and goods tied up in buffalo skins, across, while we followed, some swimming and others in skin boats towed by men and women in the water. I was ferried over by two women and a man, the former swimming with cords between their teeth attached to the boat, and the latter pushing behind, by which means I was safely landed on the shore. Here I found a new party of Indians, who while our party was crossing the river had stolen three of my horses. Continuing our course we crossed a creek on a raft near the White-haired village, which was deserted, and in the evening of the third day after passing the Shoshona, we crossed the Missouri line. Here my brother exclaimed,—"Thank God we are once more in the United States." We encamped for the night, and lay down in fancied security, without setting a guard, and in the morning discovered that a large number of the horses and mules had been stolen. We had not seen any Indians for three days, but had been followed by the prowling Osages, who had now effected their designs upon us. Thirty-eight of my best horses and mules were missing. We followed the thieves to the White-haired village, and found that they had crossed the creek on our rafts, and were now beyond all pursuit. We returned and proceeded on with the remains of my drove. Our next stopping place was Chouteau's trading house on the north side of the Osage river, about six miles from our last, where we found a hospitable reception from the French traders. McKnight and I went to the factory or Government store a few miles above on the river, where we saw a few Indians, the factor, and an interpreter, who advised me to go, or send some persons back to Grand River for my horses, where they would probably be found. I hired him and an Indian, for forty dollars, to return with one of my men to recover the stolen property. In a few days they came back with the news that the thieves had hastened on towards Chermout's village on the Arkansas, where they had probably concealed my chattels. Giving them up for lost, I returned to Chouteau's establishment and endeavored to obtain a skiff for descending the river. Most of my remaining horses were sore on the back or jaded so much as to be unable to carry any burdens. We learned from a blacksmith that there was a missionary station on the river a few miles above, where a good skiff which he had made, could be procured. The two McKnights, the blacksmith, and myself, went up to the station, where we found a small village of about fifty inhabitants, old and young, and a dozen houses. A fine water mill was going up on the opposite or south side of the river. We found the owners of the skiff, related to them our wants and misfortunes, and requested the privilege of buying their skiff. They doubted if they could spare the skiff. We went down to the river and examined the subject of our negotiation, which was a rough made article, of the value in St. Louis of about three dollars. "We have no stuff to make another with, should we let this go," said one of the missionaries. "I have some plank," said the blacksmith, "the same as this was made of, that you may have to make another if you wish it. These men," continued he, "have been very unfortunate, and by letting them have the skiff you will do an act of charity. They can't travel without it;" and I told them I would give any reasonable price for the accommodation. "Well, said the missionary, what would you be willing to give?" Ten dollars.

"Ho, ho!—I couldn't take that for the skiff, even if I could spare it. But we can't let it go, we want it for crossing the river to the mill. I v(e)ow and declare I can't spare it." I will give you fifteen dollars, said I. "Oh no," whined the philanthropist, "we couldn't take that little, and besides I have no nails to make another with." "I will make nails for you said the blacksmith; that need not be in your way," and again the benevolent trader was headed. "But I v(e)ow I don't know how to spare it," said he. I then offered twenty dollars in specie. "Oh no," said the missionary, "the skiff is worth more than that, but I don't think we can spare it;" and here the negotiation ended, my companions protesting that I had offered too much already. We went up to the village where they had three half-breed children under instruction, and these were all their pupils or converts whom they were paid by Government to instruct—truly a disinterested company of men. Learning that we had arrived from Mexico, a number of them gathered around us with many questions concerning that country, and one asked if they were not in need of missionaries in that country, and whether much good could not be done and many converts made there Robert McKnight replied, "they would convert you into the calaboose d—nd quick, if you were to go among them—you had better stay here." We left then, shaking the dust of the town from our feet and glad to get rid of the canting sharpers. We returned to the trading post, made a few bark canoes, and proceeded down the river; part of our company being in the canoes and the rest afoot with the horses and goods. At the mouth of the Osage, Rogers, the ferryman, informed us that at the village of Cote Sans Desans, on the opposite side of the Missouri, I could procure some perogues of the French inhabitants there. I crossed over to the village and purchased a canoe and perogue for sixteen dollars—loaded them with goods, and with the McKnights I hastened forward to St. Louis. The rest of my company with the horses, joined me soon afterwards. I here heard that Glenn had sold out his fur and gone to Cincinnati. As I remarked before, he has been among the missing to me ever since. His note I will sell for one per cent. on the principal.

I learned on the morning of my arrival at St. Louis, that Col. Graham, the Indian Agent, had just started for the Osage country, to pay out annuities to the Osages. The two McKnights pursued and overtook him—gave him a written statement of my losses by that tribe, and claimed compensation, which he undertook to obtain for me. The Osages delivered up twenty-seven of my horses and mules, and said that these were all they had taken. The agent took their words for the fact against the written and sworn statements of the McKnights, which could have been corroborated by the oaths of my whole company, and neglected to retain the amount of what they had cost me in Santa Fe, which was forty dollars each, out of the annuities of the Osages, which were then paid in money. He brought on the twenty-seven, which he recovered as far as the Osage river in Missouri, where he left them, at the house of a man named Rogers, who wrote to inform me in the winter following that they were dying with hunger. Col. Graham had turned them out to go at large, and when two men whom I sent for them, arrived, only sixteen could be found. Four mules which were unable to travel were left, and only twelve horses and mules were brought back; to recover which I expended much more than their value. The agent, Col. Graham, was greatly culpable in not retaining the whole value of the horses stolen, out of the annuities of the Osages. The claim was proved and might and ought to have been secured by him.

In the latter part of July, 1822, I arrived at my home

in Monroe county, Illinois, after an absence of fifteen months. I was supposed to be dead by many, and my family were entertaining the most alarming apprehensions for me. The husband and the father only, can appreciate the joy and rejoicing which my coming occasioned, and the cordial welcome I received. After the hardships, exposures and wearing anxieties which I had endured for more than a year, I needed repose and relaxation, and I hoped to enjoy them for a short time. But in this hope I was disappointed. My creditors swarmed around me like bees, and were as clamorous as a drove of hungry wolves. I had brought from Santa Fe about $2500, the sole proceeds of my stock of $12000 with which I had left St. Louis the year before. This sum I immediately paid on my debts, and offered all my remaining property to my creditors; but they wanted money. The Sheriff, the Marshal, and Constables immediately beset me on every side, and seized and sold almost every thing of mine that was levyable. I worked and struggled bravely to emerge from this thick cloud of difficulties. I drove a mill and distillery, and fattened a drove of hogs for which I could find no sale. The way was dark before me and I found more real trouble and corroding care in getting out of debt than I had experienced among the savages. Man in civilized society frequently requires more firmness of mind, constancy, fortitude, and real strength of character than in the most critical and dangerous crisis of a savage state. The poor man, struggling bravely against an accumulation of debt and difficulty. I have always thought, is entitled to more respect than the military chieftain, whose courage is only inflamed by the excitements of war and ambition. Peace has its victories as well as war, and a high state of civilization as it has stronger temptations to evil and higher though less pressing incitements to exertion, so it requires more energy and determined resolu-

tion of mind than any other condition of human existence. Many a brave and true man in the peaceful shades
of private life will receive a meed of honor equal to
that of

> Great men battling with the storms of fate
> And greatly falling with a falling State.

CHAPTER VI

Endeavors to get out of debt—Proposition of John McKnight—
Preparations for another expedition—Journey to the Arkansas—
Ascent of the Canadian and North Fork—Hunting Bears, Elks,
&c.—Fort commenced—Conversation with McKnight and his
departure in search of Camanches—Continued ascent of the
Canadian North Fork—A new Fort—Return of Potter and Ivy—
Robert McKnight goes out in search of his brother—He returns
with Indians—Charges them with the murder of his brother—
I go out to the Camanche village—Incidents there—A council—
The One Eyed Chief—The whole band start for the Fort—A
guard placed over me—Encampment—The One Eyed adopts me
as his brother—He changes my relations with his tribes—Catching wild horses—Arrival at the Fort—Fright of some "brave"
men—Trade—A robbery—The One Eyed punishes the thieves—
Fate of John McKnight—Mourning stopped—Indian customs—A
dance—A case of arbitration by the One Eyed—Indian horsemanship—Parting with the Chiefs—Conversation with Alsarea—
The horse Checoba—A Bucephalus.

SEEING NO WAY of extricating myself from debt by any
regular employment at home, I cast about for some other
means of self preservation. John McKnight, who was to
me a true and faithful friend, went to the mines to obtain
for me a lucrative situation, but without success. He then
proposed to make another venture among the Camanches,
and endeavor to obtain from them the fulfilment of Cordaro's promise to remunerate my losses among his countrymen. McKnight was sanguine of success, and I fell in
with his proposal. We procured goods in St. Louis, on
credit, to the value of $5500, shipped them on a keel boat,
and the two McKnights, John and Robert, with eight

123

men, started with them in the fall of 1822 for the mouth
of the Canadian, where I was to meet them in the winter
following. I went by land to the place of rendezvous,
with a company of twelve men, through the towns of
Batesville, (now Fredericktown,) St. Francisville, and the
Cherokee country, and joined McKnight in the latter part
of February. We had five horses with packs and travelled
the whole route afoot. McKnight had awaited us about
six weeks. We found him with the boat frozen up, about
four miles above the Canadian, on the north side of the
Arkansas and about thirty miles below Barbour's trading
house. On going up to Barbour's, McKnight and I found
that he had secured the goods which we had *cached* on
the island above in my former trip; but that the flour was
damaged when he took it down to his house. He was just
starting, when we arrived, for New Orleans, with furs
and peltry on my keel-boat, which I had left with him
the year before, and he promised to pay me, on his return, for the boat and goods. I never saw him again: he
died on this trip in New Orleans. The ice being now
gone, and our boat released, we prepared for ascending
the Canadian. Robert McKnight with most of the men,
descended the Arkansas with the boat, to enter the Canadian four miles below, while John, who was seldom
separated from me, with the horses and a few men crossed
the point and awaited them. After joining them we travelled
in sight of the boat till we passed the falls about twenty-
five miles from the mouth, when we struck into the best
farming country I had ever seen; a beautiful land of
prairies and woods in fine proportion. Below the falls we
passed a very salt spring. Elk, buffalo, deer, wild turkeys
and black bears were very abundant, and we fared on
the fat of the land. The soil is extremely fertile, judging
from the heavy grass of the prairies and the large and
valuable timber of the woods, which were composed of

walnut, ash, hackberry, spice, pawpaw, and oaks of a very heavy growth and of every species. The Canadian is very crooked and bounded by extensive bottoms. After travelling five days through this fine region, we struck the North Fork of the Canadian at its mouth. This river, like the other, is exceedingly crooked, and numerous rapids greatly obstruct its navigation. Our ascent was slow and difficult, and the boat twice stopped at night within a hundred yards of our encampment of the night before, owing to the irregular course of the stream. Our progress in the boat was at length stopped entirely by a rapid which we could not ascend. We made fast the boat to trees with strong ropes, put our bear and deer skins into it, and buried the heaviest hardware in the ground, where it remains probably to this day, as I never returned to its place of concealment. We made three perouges, into which we put our remaining goods except such as could be packed on the horses, and with them, we continued our ascent of the Canadian North Fork. Game of every kind known to the country was extremely plenty. We killed on this and the main river about twenty black bears, all of which we found in the hollow of trees where they had remained in a torpid state all winter. In one tree four were found, a she and three yearling cubs, which the men killed with axes, after felling the tree and stopping up the top to prevent their escape. After proceeding with our perogues about ten days the game became scarce and the company began to suffer from want of food. We stopped and all sallied out to hunt: the first day furnished but one wild turkey. The second and third days produced nothing more, the turkey subsisting us all for three days. John McKnight and I then went about ten miles in search of game, and found a bear's track, but our pursuit of the bear was unsuccessful. Returning by a different route from that by which we came, we descried a herd of elk, lying down in the prairie. We crept on our hands and knees in the short grass to within two hundred yards of them, when one discovered us, leaped up, snorted and brought the rest to their feet. I instantly fired and wounded one, which we found and killed, and returned with a part of the meat to our companions, who were feasting on a wild horse. In the morning, after bringing in the remainder of my elk, we pursued our journey and in a few days the game, became plentiful. We had hitherto travelled through a very fertile and beautiful country, which will in a few years teem with a dense population. The prairies are interspersed with valuable woodland, and will make as fine a farming country as any in the Union. We now reached the vast and sterile prairie west of the Cross-Timbers, through the northern end of which we had passed, and we commenced our journey over the boundless plains beyond them. This is the region designated on the maps as the Great American Desert, though it is very different from those plains of sand in the Old World which bear that name. A short grass grows here, but no timber except the cottonwood and willows in the bends of the rivers. Our path had before lain through fine groves of oak, walnut and ash as we issued from one prairie and entered another, but now one vast plain extending on all sides to the horizon, presented no object to relieve the vision.

We soon discovered trails of Indians and came upon a deserted camp of what seemed a Camanche war *party* about five hundred strong. As we proceeded, the Indian *"sign"* increased. We next struck an Osage camp, also deserted, which seemed to have been made a few weeks before by a war party or a horse stealing party of Osages on their route northward from a plundering expedition against the Camanches. The country, as we proceeded, became more and more sterile, the grass shorter and the

timber on the river banks smaller and more scarse than
before. Travelling on, through a country nearly destitute
of vegetation, in about ten days after passing the Osage
camp, we arrived at the place of encampment of an immense Indian force in the summer previous, as we judged
from the signs on the ground. The river had now became
too shallow to be navigated any further without great difficulty, even by perogues. Here we stopped and commenced the building of a Fort. One of the men, now a near
neighbor of mine, Justus Varnum, had taken a cold, so
severe that it affected his hip and back and prevented
him from walking. He was conveyed up the river in a
perogue for several weeks previous to our stopping, and
he had to be carried every night in a blanket from the
boat to the fires of the camp, and back again to the boats
in the morning. One of the men, when we had stopped
to build a Fort, killed a large rattlesnake with the entire
bodies of two prairie dogs, larger than squirrels, contained
within the stomach of his snakeship. I advised Varnum
to try out the oil of the snake and rub it on his joints as a
remedy. He applied the oil as I recommended, and in
consequence became so limber and supple as to render
walking painful to him, when I told him to stop the ap-
plications. I have frequently tried the same remedy for
stiffness of the joints and think it might be of service in
rheumatism.

The Fort being nearly completed, I proposed to go
out with two men and find the Camanches, in whose
country we then were, and who, we supposed from
"*signs*" around us, could not be very distant. John Mc-
Knight objected to my going out, saying that he or I
must remain with the men and superintend the building
of the Fort, as his brother Robert could not govern the
company. "You, James," said he, "have a family. I have
none, and therefore I can better afford to lose my life

than you. As we cannot, both of us go, you must remain."
At his urgent solicitation, I acquiesced, though unwill-
ingly, in this arrangement, and agreed with him in the
event of the river's rising before we finished the Fort, to
put the goods in the perogues, and ascend the stream a
hundred miles, after leaving a letter for him in a certain
part of the Fort. I wished to get into the heart of the
Camanche country with my goods, where I would sooner
be able to open a trade with the nation. McKnight departed according to our arrangement towards the south,
in company with Potter, Ivy, and Clark, the last of whom
was an obstinate, disaffected man, and went against the
desire of McKnight. He, poor fellow, never returned. He
found a soldier's death and a brave man's grave from the
hands of the Camanche warriors. He was my friend—
faithful and true to me—and I mourned his loss as that of
one whose place could never be supplied to me or to society. I learned soon after this, the probable circumstances attending his death. A few days after McKnight
left us, a heavy rain fell, causing the river to rise, and we
thereupon abandoned the Fort about half completed, and
with our perogues and goods ascended about the distance
agreed upon, where the low water stopped our fur-prog-
ress. We encamped and commenced a Fort in an excellent
position where the timber was abundant. We proceeded
in building the Fort as expeditiously as possible, and with
great labor soon completed it and a trading house, surrounded by stockades and defended by our swivel, which
we mounted on wheels in an angle of the Fort. Before
this, however, Potter and Ivy returned with the news that
on the ninth day after their departure they fell in with
Camanches and were conducted to one of their principal
villages, (the bands in camp, are called by that name)
and that McKnight called a counsel with their Chiefs, but
could not, for want of an interpreter, make himself well

understood; Potter knowing less of the language than was supposed. McKnight then gave them to understand that he had a good interpreter in Spanish, referring to his brother Robert, and requested leave to return to us for him, in company with one man. The Indians permitted him to start alone and kept the remaining three as hostages. They gave him five days for his journey to our camp and back to them, and he left them with the promise to return on the fifth day. After his departure, Clark made known to them by signs that McKnight's company had many guns and a cannon. This excited their fears and they gave evident symptoms of alarm. On the same day a party of Indians came in, as from a hunt, and the Americans were told that two Camanches of their village had just been killed by Osages. The whole army then decamped and removed fifteen miles further south. The three prisoners heard moaning and lamentation for the deceased in two lodges, during the whole night. For seven days they were kept awaiting McKnight, when the Indians upbraided them with his failure and pretended treachery, but permitted Potter and Ivy to go out for the Spanish interpreter. They came in much surprised that McKnight had not appeared. I instantly conjectured his fate. A man sent by me down to the unfinished Fort, returned with the information that the letter, I had left, was still there. Robert McKnight returned with Potter and Ivy to the Camanche village, and here he charged the Indians with the murder of his brother. His conduct among them was like a mad man's, storming and raging with no regard to consequences. At length they were persuaded, on the assurance that I was at the Fort, to send out forty mounted warriors, with McKnight, while the rest remained as hostages. On the third day after Robert McKnight went out, I saw an Indian on a mound, surveying our encampment. I hoisted the flag and fired the swivel, when he was soon joined by others, all splendidly mounted on the best of horses, and I noticed Robert McKnight on a mule in their midst, and guarded. They stopped on the hill as if waiting for a parley with us, and I took my pistols, placed a plume in my hat, and went out to them. McKnight pointed me to their Chief, who was a Towash, and whom I invited into the Fort. He advanced with his band very cautiously and when within two hundred yards of the Fort alighted and walked around to the river bank, looking for some traces of the Osages. Finding none, but still suspicious, he entered the Fort and examined every nook and corner of it, and then looked at my goods. He appeared satisfied and called to his company, who rode up; but before they would enter the Fort, they searched up and down the river bank for vestiges of their enemies. I entertained them with boiled buffalo meat, and while they were eating I enquired of McKnight if Big Star was at the village. He said no, and that these were another tribe whom I had not seen before. I remarked to him that I recognised one Indian among them, whom I had certainly seen before, and had endeavored to hire as an interpreter, at the village where we were robbed in my former trip. His name said I is *Whon*, (from the Spanish John). As I mentioned his name the Indian raised his head, looked at me and instantly cast his eyes on the ground. The Chief asked the interpreter what I said, and on hearing it, asked me where I had seen *Whon*. When I had told him of our former acquaintance, he and Whon conversed together a moment, when Whon arose and threw his arms around my neck and asked in Spanish how I had been. McKnight asked why he had not spoken to *him* in Spanish as he spoke it so well. He said he had come to see if I was really the man spoken of by John McKnight and that he had been commanded not to speak Spanish or let us know who he was. John McKnight had told them as plainly as he could by Potter, that I had visited their country the year before, and had now returned because I had promised Cordaro that I would do so, for the purpose of trading with them. The Chief now told me that the nation would not come to the Fort to trade, on account of the Osages, and I agreed to go with them in the morning with goods to their village. McKnight proposed in the night to put all the goods into the boats and escape down the river, as they had undoubtedly killed his brother and might do the same deed upon us all. He was an impulsive, passionate man, with but little cool reflection. His courage in the midst of danger was of the highest order and perfectly unyielding, but he was unfit for a leader or guide in critical situations, requiring coolness and presence of mind. I refused to attempt an escape as utterly impracticable, and the height of injustice to the men who were in custody with the Camanches. In the morning I started alone with four mules loaded with goods and escorted by the Indians under Alsarea, for the village, where we arrived in the evening and were met by the head Chief about two miles from the town. He appeared friendly and took the goods and deposited them in his lodge. Potter and the other hostages were all in safety and had been well treated. They informed me that my old and formidable enemy the One-Eyed Chief was in the village. On the next morning, I prepared for trading by making presents, according to custom, of knives, tobacco, cloths for breech garments, &c., which, though a large heap when together, made a small appearance when divided among all this band. The trade then began. They claimed twelve articles for a horse. I made four yards of British strouding at $5.50 per yard and two yards of calico at 62½ cents to count three, and a knife, flint, tobacco, looking-glass, and other small articles made up the compliment. They brought to me some horses for which I refused the stipulated price. They then produced others, which were really fine animals, worth at least $100 each in St. Louis. I bought seventeen of these, but would not take any more at the same price, the rest being inferior. The refusal enraged the Chief, who said I must buy them, and on my presisting in my course, drove away the Indians from around me, and left me alone. After a short time he returned with a request that I should buy some buffalo and beaver skins, to which I acceded. He went away and the woman soon returned with the fur and skins, of which I bought a much larger quantity than I wished then to have on my hands. The Chief again came up and drove away all my women customers, and I was again left alone with the three who had come with McKnight. No Indian came near me for the rest of the day, and I sauntered around the village and amused myself as well as I could till night-fall. During this time and most of the night before I had heard moaning, lamentations and weeping from two lodges in the outskirts of the village, on account of the two Indians, killed, their countrymen said, by Osages, but who undoubtedly met their death from the hands of John McKnight, fighting desperately in his own defence. In the evening the old Chief in whose lodge I staid, entered my tent with five old Indians, and all with a grave and solemn air sat themselves down in silence. The Chief, who was a little, low flat headed and simple looking old man, soon arose, took a pipe which he filled with tobacco and presented it to each of his companions in succession. He passed me by unnoticed and all regarded me with lowering brows. This I knew portended evil, and I feared the worst. After they had all smoked, the Chief made them a speech in Camanche, which I knew nothing of, and then turned to me and spoke in Spanish fluently. I understood perfectly, every word he uttered and heard him with intense interest. He asked when I was going away. I replied that I was an American and had come from my own country, a great distance, to trade with his people, because I had promised the Chief Cordaro the year before that I would come; that I had done according to my promise and brought them guns, powder, knives, tomahawks, and other things which I knew his people wanted. The Chief replied that they did not want to trade, but wished me to go immediately out of their country. "We are going to the Nachatoshauwa, (Red River) and you must leave us." I offered to accompany them. "No, no," said he, "our meat is scarce, the game is scarce; you must not go; away! away! (waving his hand) go out of our country." I felt that my fate and that of my men rested with this council, and that as they arose friendly or hostile, should we live or die the death of John McKnight. This old Chief evidently wished me to start on my way back to the Fort, and intended then to pursue me with his warriors and make my scalp and goods the prizes of the race or the spoil of the battle. I concealed all alarm in my demeanor, and reaching back as I sat to a tobacco keg, I broke off twelve plugs, and took out of a box six wampums, which are strings of long beads, variously colored, and greatly prized by the Indians. I then took out my *calama* or Indian pipe, and slowly filled it with tobacco, saying in an under tone and a musing manner, as if speaking to myself as much as to them, I shall have to go back to my own country after coming all this distance to trade with my red brethren, and when I tell the people of my nation how our red brothers have treated me, they will never come into this country. I have bought every thing that my red brothers want for war or for peace, guns and powder and ball, and clothes for their women, and now they are driving me out of their country like a spy or a thief, instead of a friend and brother as I am. When I had lighted the pipe, I presented it with one hand and the two plugs of tobacco and a wampum with the other, to the Chief, saying to him, this is better than you get from the Spaniards. I well knew the sacredness of this offer, and that the Indian dare not offend the Great Spirit by refusing a present of tobacco and wampum, even from his bitterest enemy. The Chief hesitated long, but at last slowly raised his hand, took my presents and smoked the pipe. Giving one puff to the skies, one to the earth, two to the winds and waters on the right and left, and then a few whiffs on his own and our accounts, he returned the pipe to me. In the same manner I presented it to an old Indian who sat beside me, and who kept his head down and his eyes shut. I held the presents close to his face for some time, when the Chief spoke to him, and he slowly raised his hand without looking up, took the presents, smelled of the tobacco, pressed it to his heart and raised his head with a smile. Then white man had gained the ascendant. The scene changed and all was friendly welcome where before was nothing but menacing and frowning coldness. All the others now received my presents and we smoked out the pipe in the friendship and confidence of brothers. The Chief then very earnestly asked me if I had seen the Osages. I said, I have not, but you know that this is their hunting ground and they may be in the country. They said they knew this, and some further conversation established our intimacy on a firm footing. The Chief then went out into the village and proclaimed in a loud voice that all should prepare to go next morning, over to the Canadian, to trade with the Tabbahoes, their white friends. Before this we were called Americanos, which was a less familiar and friendly appellation than the former. The proclamation was continued by the herald on horseback till late at night, each sentence ending with

Tabbahoes. "Get up your horses and make ready to go over to the white man's and trade with the Tabbahoes. They have come a great way and brought us many good things—the Tabbahoes are good." This was loudly sounded before my lodge, and throughout the village all was preparation, joy and gladness.

About sundown Potter entered our lodge with the greatest alarm depicted in his countenance, and gave me a gun barrel which the One Eyed Chief had just thrown down before him, and told him to carry to me. This was the last man on earth that I desired to see, for I regarded him my most deadly and most dangerous enemy, who had probably killed John McKnight and was now seeking my blood. I asked Potter what else he said, and as he answered, "nothing more," he looked out and exclaimed, "there he is now, sitting on his horse. What shall I say to him?" I walked out to my old enemy and offered my hand. He took it with a steady and piercing look into my very soul; I returned his glance with an air of calm consideration and requested him to alight and enter my lodge. He did so, after delivering his horse to a bystander. In the lodge I motioned to him to be seated on a heap of skins. He sat down in silence and deep gravity. I lighted and smoked out the pipe with him in utter silence, and then took a silver gorget or breast-plate, and with a ribbon attached I hung it around his neck and placed two silver arm bands just above the elbows, and two upon his wrists. The warrior submitted to all this in passive and abstracted silence, as if unconscious of what I was doing. I then put two plugs of tobacco, a knife and wampum, in his lap, while he preserved the rigid and inflexible appearance of a statue. I again lighted the pipe and smoked with him, when he arose, without a word, went out, and rode off with great rapidity

In the morning, all was confusion and busy activity in

the village, and one half of the band started for the Fort before me. I followed with the three men, and without a guard. In crossing a creek near the village, a horse became entangled and I told the men to hasten on and take care of the goods, while I loosened the horse, which I did, and on crossing the creek found sixty men drawn up in two lines on either side and who closed around me as I approached them. I asked the Chief—who was Alasarea, the Towash—what he meant by this conduct. "Kesh, kesh, kinsable," said he, "stop, stop; who knows but you are taking us over to your Fort to have us all killed by the Osages?" I asked him if he ever knew me to lie. He said he had not, but he knew that the Spaniards were great liars. That may be said I, but the Americans never lie. "I do not know the Americans, said he, but I know that the Spaniards are great liars. I then reiterated my bold assertion of American veracity and said, when your tribe robbed me on the South Fork and I promised to visit your village on the Canadian and trade with you, did I not go as I promised? "Yes," said the Chief. And when Cordaro came to see me in Santa Fe, I promised him to go home and return with goods this year to your country. You know this, and have I not performed my promise? "Yes you have," he said, and asked if I had not seen Osages. I told him I had not. With my words he appeared but partially satisfied, and reluctantly proceeded with me under a strong guard, but promised that my mules, horses, and goods, should be secured. In this manner I traveled all day, during which time the One Eyed spoke not a word to me. Late in the evening we crossed the Canadian and encamped on the bank. I was marched to the head Chief's lodge, where I found the men at liberty and my horses, &c., in good order. I went into the lodge to prepare for passing the night as comfortably as possible, and was engaged in looking at my goods, when my enemy the

One Eyed rode up and to my surprise addressed me fluently in the Spanish language. This was the first time he had ever spoken to me. The man who had done me more injury than any other human being, from whose hands I had twice, narrowly escaped a bloody death, such, as I had every reason to suppose, McKnight had suffered from him—this man spoke to me kindly and invited me to go with him to his lodge. Suspecting treachery, I was loath to accept the invitation, and while I was hesitating, the old Chief came up, and called me to him. On hearing what the One Eyed wanted, he told me not to go, because "he is a bad man." Again the One Eyed came to me and repeated his request, which I refused peremptorily, and he walked a few steps away with an impatient, angry air, then suddenly turning around, he fixed his piercing black eye intently upon me, walked up to me and implored, with a beseeching look and tones, that I should go with him to his lodge. I saw that he was unarmed, while I had two pistols, a tomahawk, and knife in my belt, and could anticipate the first hostile motion from him; also, that we were four men, in the midst of three thousand, and entirely at their mercy should they design to do us any injury. I offered to visit the One Eyed on the following morning. "No, no," said he, "come now— oh! do come—come with me," in a tone of supplication. I, at length, yielded and walked on towards his lodge, till the village dogs attacked me so furiously that he was obliged to dismount from his horse to my defence. He then offered me a seat on his horse, in front of him. I mounted behind him as the safest position, when he applied the whip and flew with me to his lodge, which we entered and were received by one of his wives with smiles and glad welcoming. A wife of the One Eyed took his horse as he alighted. In the lodge I took a seat opposite that of the Chief, and, facing his arms which hung over his bed or cot of buffalo robe. I could thus watch his motions and foil any murderous design that he might manifest, by shooting him on the spot and making my escape on his horse. He lighted a pipe, however, and we smoked till his wife brought in some buffalo meat, of which we ate, while she apologised to me very kindly and politely for its poorness. "We have no marrow to cook with the meat and the buffalo are poor. It is the best we have, and you are welcome," said this charming squaw. The One Eyed only urged me to eat heartily, and when the repast was over, we again smoked the pipe in silence. Shaking the ashes into his hand, he slowly raised his head, looked into my face and asked if I knew him. I replied, yes. "Where did you first see me?" On the Salt Fork of the Canadian. "Where, the second time?" At the village on the Canadian Fork. "Did you know then that I wanted to kill you?" Yes I knew it. "True, I sought your life, and but for Big Star, the head Chief of the Ampireka band, I should have killed you and your men. I knew that you were traders with the Osages; you had their horses, their ropes, their skins, their saddles. The Osages had come and taken about two hundred of our horses, and I went out with a war party to recover them and punish the robbers. We found them, and fought a battle with them, in which my brother was killed. My brother was a great warrior, a good hunter and a good man. I loved my brother." He then talked in a strain of mournful eulogy on his brother, while the tears coursed down his face, and he ended in violent weeping. Recovering himself, he said that he had gone out on a second expedition to revenge his brother's death, when he overtook me on the Salt Fork of the Canadian, and there intended to murder our company. He then put the ashes which he held in his hand, on the ground, and taking a handful of earth from the fire place, covered the ashes with it, patting it three times with his hand. Another handful he used in the same manner, and then a third, during which time he moaned and wept violently; so much so that I was uneasy for my own safety in this outbreak of grief. He then looked up with an altered countenance, and exclaimed, "there, I have now buried my brother; but I have found another. I will take you for my brother;" and in a transport of feeling he embraced me with the words, "my brother, my brother." He then placed a charm around my neck, which he said would protect me from all enemies. It had been his brother's, but when going into his last battle with the Osages, the owner left it behind with his blanket, and *therefore,* was killed. He then asked if the old Chief had tried to dissuade me from coming to his lodge, and on hearing that he had, he said: "He is an old fool: he does not know whether he will kill you or not, and he wants me to be your enemy, so that he may have my assistance should he determine to destroy you. If he dreams a good dream he is pleasant and friendly to you; if a bad one, he is grum and gloomy and wishes me to join him in killing you. He is an old fool. He and his men expect to get back all the horses that you bought of them at the village, and that was the reason of their selling so many of the best to you; but you are now safe, you and your property. They shall not harm you or take back any of the horses. Though my men are few, yet every Indian in the nation fears me. They shall treat you well. I will describe you to all the nation, so that whenever you come among us you shall be safe from all danger. I will tell them you are my brother." We then conversed on various subjects, the battles he had fought, his ideas of religion, &c. He bore proofs of his courage on his person, in five wounds; some of them large and dangerous. An arrow had pierced his left eye and a lance his side; but owing to the charm, or *"medicine,"* which he wore, his enemies had been unable to kill him. He had been christened in the Spanish country, and said, "I believe as you do in the Great Spirit. If I do well I shall go to a good place and be happy. If I do badly I shall go to the bad place and be miserable.

On taking leave, I requested him to accompany me to keep off the dogs. Take my horse said he. But how shall I return him? "You will not return him, you will keep him my brother—keep him in remembrance of me." I left with a lighter heart than I had brought to the lodge of the One Eyed Chief. I counted much on the benefit of his friendship, and subsequent events proved that I did not overrate its advantages. I met the old Chief on my return, who asked me if I had bought the horse of the One Eyed. His countenance fell on hearing the manner of my acquiring the animal, and he requested me to exchange for a fine spotted war horse of his own, and then offered to give two for that of "my brother's." I refused the insidious proposal, which was intended only to sow dissension between me and my new friend, and the Chief appeared very angry at his failure.

Early the following morning, I saw the One Eyed Chief coming with two ribs of buffalo meat, and calling to me moneta, moneta, (my brother) "your sister has sent some buffalo meat for your breakfast." The Chiefs of the army, who were all present and heard this unexpected salutation, looked at each other in astonishment at this extraordinary treatment of me by their greatest brave, who so lately appeared so implacable in his hostility to me. Their conduct towards me and the men immediately changed. No guard was, after this, kept over us, and we were treated with respect and kindness. My powerful "brother," put a new face on our affairs and very probably saved us from the fate of McKnight. We now proceeded towards the Fort, the One Eyed riding by my side and talking very good humoredly and with great animation on a variety of topics. About the middle of the day I noticed preparations making by the warriors as for battle. I asked the One Eyed what this signified, and before he could reply, Alasarea rode up and exclaimed, "Osages, Osages, a heap," and asked me whether I would stay or go over to them. I will stay said I. "Will you fight for us?" I will, said I, and the One Eyed laughed and said they were only wild horses that had caused the alarm. I ascended a mound with him, whence I could observe the manner of catching these animals. In an incredible short time one hundred were captured and tamed so as to be nearly as subject to their masters as domestic horses reared on a farm. A small party of less than a hundred well mounted Indians were in ambush, while a multitude scattered themselves over the prairie in all directions and drove the wild horses to the place where the others were concealed, which was a deep ravine. As soon as the wild drove were sufficiently near, these last rushed among them and every Indian secured his horse with his lassoo or noosed rope, which he threw around the neck of the animal, and by a sudden turn brought him to the ground and there tied his heels together. This was the work of a few minutes, during which both horses and men were intermingled together in apparently inextricable confusion. The whole drove was taken at the first onset, except a fine black stud which flew like the wind, pursued by a hundred Indians, and in about two hours was brought back tamed and gentle. He walked close by the Indian who had captured him, and who led him by a rope and wished to sell him to me. I feared his wild look and dilated eye, but his Indian master and protector said he was gentle and gave me the end of the rope with which he led him, when the noble animal immediately came near to me as to a new friend and master. He seemed by his manner to have ratified the transfer and chosen me in preference to the Indian. In twenty-four hours after their capture these horses became tamed and ready for use, and keep near to their owners as their only friends. I could perceive little difference between them and our farm horses. The Indians use their fleetest horses for catching the wild ones, and throw the *lassoo* with great dexterity over their necks, when by turning quickly round and sometimes entangling their feet in the rope, they throw them on the ground, and then tie their legs together two and two, after which they release the neck from the tightened noose which in a short time would produce death by strangling. The sport is attended with the wildest excitement, and exceeds in interest and enjoyment all other sports of the chase that I ever saw.

A thunder shower now blew up, and the army stretched their lodges and encamped. After the shower, a war party of about seven hundred men, under the command of Alasarea, started with me for the Fort, where we arrived about sundown. Each Indian was armed with a short gun, a bow and arrows, and a lance; some had pistols, and each had two horses, one of which he rode for marching, and one, his war horse, which he led, for the battle. Their appearance was formidable indeed as they approached the Fort, and somewhat alarmed the garrison. They encamped for that night outside of the Fort, and in the morning I made them presents with which they were greatly pleased. At about ten o'clock the whole Camanche army came in sight, when some of my company were still more alarmed than they had been the day before. Several who before starting, talked boastingly of making a razor strap of an Indian's skin, now lay in their tents quaking with fear and sweating cold drops. This was the first Indian army they had ever seen, and their courage fast melted away before the spectacle. Come out, said I to

them, now is your time to get a razor strap. The Camanches encamped in front of the Fort, on a space a mile
and a half in length and about half a mile wide, and
exhibited a friendly disposition. I traded with them for
horses, mules, beaver fur, and buffalo robes. The former
I sent as fast as I bought them, to a drove about a mile
from the village, under charge of three men. On the
morning of the third day four Indians, armed, went to
the drove and took four of the best horses, in spite of the
resistance of the guard, who were intimidated by their
violence. I immediately went to my "brother," the One
Eyed, and informed him of the robbery. He mounted his
horse, with whip in hand, and in about two hours returned
with two of the stolen horses. In the afternoon he brought
back a third, and at night, came up with the fourth. His
whip was bloody, and his face distorted with rage. He was
in a mood to make men tremble before him, when none
but the boldest spirits would dare to cross his path or
oppose his will. After he had left the last horse with me,
I heard his voice in every part of the camp, proclaiming
what, the interpreter told me was a warning for the protection of my property. "Your horses are yours," said he,
"to sell or keep as you please; but when you once sell
them you cannot take them back. My brother has come
from afar to trade with you and brought things that are
good for you; and when you have sold him your horses
and got your pay, you must not take them back." After
this I was not molested again in a smiliar manner. The
One Eyed Chief spent much of his time in my trading
house, and assisted me by his advice and influence over
the Indians. He allowed me to judge of the horses for
myself, but selected the buffalo robes for me and settled
their prices. I bought many more of the latter than I
brought back with me and might have purchased thousands. One plug of tobacco, a knife and a few strings of

beads, in all worth but little more than a dime, bought one of these valuable skins or "rober," worth at least five dollars in any of the States.

The Indians had with them a great many young Spaniards as prisoners, one of whom, an excellent interpreter, wished me to purchase him. I offered the price of ten horses for him, but without success. I gave him many presents, which, he said, his masters took from him as soon as they saw them, and he requested me to give him no more, as said he, "it is of no use." He was an intelligent and interesting boy.

The Indians spent much time in drilling and fighting mock battles. Their skill and discipline would have made our militia dragoons blush for their inferiority. They marched and countermarched, charged and retreated, rapidly and in admirable order. Their skill in horsemanship is truly wonderful, and I think, is not surpassed by that of the Cossacks or Mamelukes. I frequently put a plug of tobacco on the ground for them to pick up when riding at full speed. A dozen horsemen would start in a line for the prize, and if the leader missed it, the second or third was always successful in seizing it, when he took the rear to give the others fair chance in the next race.

There were six Pawnees from the river Platte, among these Camanches; one of whom came to me and said he knew me. Where did you ever see me? "At the Osage village, said he, when you were buying horses." I then recollected that this Pawnee with several others had come into the village to make a treaty. He knew O'Fallan, of Council Bluff, very well, and gave me some news of the Upper Missouri, and the traders there. He went off and soon returned with several Camanches, and again talked about the Osages and my trading with them. Perceiving his treacherous purpose, I made no reply to his remarks which were as follows: "I saw you with the Osages;

you bought horses of the Osages. Do you know where Osage village is? Is it not here?" marking on the ground the courses of the Arkansas, the Grand and the Verdigris rivers, and pointing to the place of their enemies' village. At last I told him I knew nothing about the Osages or their villages, which seemed to enrage him greatly, and he reiterated his assertions about having met me among the hereditary enemies of the Pawnees and Camanches. Seeing the evil suspicions produced by his talk among the Indians, and the necessity of putting down the bad report without delay, I went to my "brother" and told him the Pawnee was setting his countrymen against me. He immediately went with me to the head Chief's lodge and had my Pawnee enemy brought before him. Fixing his dark eye upon him, the One Eyed Chief regarded him a moment in silence, and then said, "we have treated you well ever since you came among us. You lied to us when you said that you had seen the 'white haired man' (meaning John McKnight) at the village of the Osages. And now you say you have seen my brother, too, among the Osages. This is all a lie. You are trying to make mischief between our people and my brother, and if you say any thing more against him I will drive you out of the nation. You shall not stay with us." The Pawnee trembled under this rebuke and walked off in silence, with the manner of a whipped spaniel. I heard no more from him.

On one occasion my "brother" asked permission to bring, in the evening, a party of his friends into the Fort to dance, and I consenting to the proposal, a party of forty, headed by the One Eyed, entered the Fort and danced for several hours, to their own singing and the sound of bells on a wand, carried by their leader. They were gorgeously attired in the height of Indian fashion and *bon ton*. They wore eagle and owl feathers, and were gaudily painted in every conceivable manner. The One

Eyed wore a showy head dress of feather work, from under which, the false hair fell to the ground; they all danced with wonderful agility and grace, and kept time better than most of dancers in more civilized and fashionable life. At the close they danced backward out of the gate, the Chief in front driving them with his wand, and they, in compliment to their host, feigning reluctance to go. With a loud shout of pleasure they at last went out together with regularity and order.

At night we were aroused by shouting and singing on all sides of the Fort, and we took our arms to repel an attack. I saw hundreds of Indians, most of them young men, clambering up the sides of the Fort and trying the doors to get in. The noise suddenly ceased and in the morning the One Eyed told me that the young men had taken the opportunity when the old men were asleep to improve their acquaintance with me and to get some presents of tobacco as the dancing party had done in the evening before, and that he had quelled the disturbance and driven them off. I heard among this party, both here and at the village where I first met them, the sound of moaning and loud wailing in two lodges, from a short time before sun set till dark. I had made a present of a gorget and arm bands to the Chief who befriended me so much on the Salt Fork of the Canadian in my former expedition, and who was now in the village. A young Indian came to me, one evening, with the gorget and arm bands as a token, and requested me to go and see this Chief in his tent. I went with the young man towards the tent whence the sound of weeping was heard, and when within thirty steps, the messenger stopped and looked at my feet. I noticed that he was bare-footed; he took off my shoes, and with me approached the Chief, who was sitting in front of his lodge with bare feet, like the spectators who were standing deferentially around; and on

the ground I saw two women and two girls, also bare-
footed and smeared over the heads and faces, with mud
and ashes. These were the same, whose voices I had heard
on first entering the Camanche village. They were now
rolling on the ground from side to side and weeping violently. Occasionally they scattered ashes over their heads,
and after short intervals of quiet, arising from exhaustion,
they would burst out afresh in irrepressible fits of weeping and sobbing. The Chief arose, took me aside, and said
that I could make these women stop crying. On my enquiring how I could do this, he replied, "by covering
them with cloth;" meaning calico. I went to the store and
got four pieces of calico, with which I returned, and covered each with a piece. The Chief now spoke to them in
his language, and appeared to console them, and remonstrated against any further exhibition of grief. Their crying gradually subsided into deep, long drawn sobs and
hiccoughs, like those of children after violent weeping.
From this night forth I heard their lamentations no more,
and a few Indians who had heretofore been cold and
distant, now became friendly to me. I concluded that
McKnight, in fighting for his life, had killed the husbands
of the women and fathers of the two girls who were thus
lamenting, and that they required a token of friendship
from me as an atonement and sign of reconciliation. The
Indians had now discovered their mistake; that in killing
McKnight they had destroyed a friend instead of an
enemy, and all regarded me more kindly on account of
their own injustice to my friend. The One Eyed Chief,
who was probably foremost in the murder, had taken me
to his heart as his only brother, and was now ready to
die for me, to atone for depriving me of my bosom friend,
McKnight—"the white haired Tabbaho." The Pawnee's
tale of having seen McKnight at the Osage village, was,
I suppose, the reason for dispatching him; and in doing

this, they had met with a desperate resistance from their
victim, who was well armed and a most excellent marks-
man. The One Eyed did all in his power to recompense
me for his loss. He was my fast friend, and exerted himself to the utmost to advance all my interests and wishes.
His wife daily sent to her "brother" some delicacy, such
as buffalo tongue, carefully cooked by herself. I began
to be reconciled to a savage life and enamored with the
simplicity of nature. Here were no debts, no Sheriffs or
Marshals; no hypocricies or false friendships. With these
simple children of the mountains and prairies, love and
hate are honestly felt and exerted in their full intensity.
No half-way passions, no interested feelings govern their
attachments to their friends. When once enlisted for or
against you, little short of Omnipotence can reverse the
Indian's position. He loves and hates with steady persist-
ence and consistency, and generally carries his first feelings regarding you, to his grave. His revenge is sure, his
love is true and disinterested. You can count upon either
with certainty, and need entertain no fear of being de-
ceived as to their operations.

A scouting war party on one occasion, brought in seven
American horses, shod and branded, a tent, a kettle, an
axe, and some other articles, which I knew must have
belonged to a trading party. They brought up the horses
to the Fort to have the shoes taken off by our blacksmith,
when I charged them with the robbery of my countrymen. They denied the charge, and said that they had
taken this spoil from a party of Osages with whom they
had had a battle, and exhibited, in proof of their operations, two scalps as those of their deadly enemies, the
Osages. I learned, at Barbour's, on my return that they
told me the truth. The Osages had robbed a Santa Fe
company and were themselves attacked in the night, by
a party they knew not of what tribe, who killed two men

and robbed them of the booty I have mentioned. It was
a fair instance of the biters being bitten, the game played
by Prince Hal upon Falstaff, who, after robbing four travellers was attacked by the Prince and plundered of his
spoil. From the warriors of this scouting party we learned
that the whole nation of Osages was very near to us;
being encamped on the Salt Fork at the distance of about
a day's journey, and they advised us to leave our present
position for one of more safety. The Camanche Chiefs
held a council of war, or grand talk, and determined to
go out and give battle to their enemies. On the next day
they sent all their women and children up the river and
went themselves, with their warriors, towards the Salt
Fork in quest of the Osages. When the last of the nation
were about going, an Indian came to me and claimed his
horse, which another Indian had sold to me without his
authority. I was about to give him the horse, when the
One Eyed came up and enquired into the case, which he
decided at once in my favor and told the claimant he
must look to the Indian who sold him, for his indemnity.
Not liking the law of this decision, I paid the Indian for
his horse, and he went away satisfied and highly pleased.
Before starting, the Chiefs in a body, came and expressed
great friendship for me and regret at leaving me as they
were compelled to do. They said they wanted the American trade, and united in requesting me to encourage my
countrymen to visit them with goods and trade with them.
Trade with the Spaniards they said, was unprofitable;
they had nothing to give them for their horses except
amunition, and this they refused to sell to the Indians
They wished the Americans to be friendly and intimate
with them, and complained bitterly that we supplied their
enemies, the Osages, with arms and amunition with
which they made war upon the Camanches. "The Osages"
said they, "get their powder, balls and guns from the

Americans, but we can get none, or very few from them; this is wrong, very wrong." The One Eyed, and several other Chiefs wished to visit their "Great Father," the President, and have a talk with him. They would have offered to accompany me to my "village" to see the Great Father, but said they, "you cannot defend us from the Osages, the Cherokees, and the Choctaws; these nations are all at war with us, and we should have to go through their country. But tell our Great Father when you go back to your village, that we want him to stop these nations from stealing our horses and killing our people, as they have been doing for many years! Tell him to protect us and send his people out to trade with us. We will not hurt his people, but will defend them when they come among us. We will be brothers with the Americans." The Chief of the Towashes told me that his tribe lived on the head waters of the Red River, and owned sixteen thousand horses, which were better than any I had bought of them. Judging from those which his warriors rode, I could believe what he said respecting the quality of their horses. He wished me to visit his tribe and trade with them. Many things did these wild Chiefs tell me to say for them to the "Great Father" when I reached my "village," and all insisted very earnestly that I should return to them in the Fall with goods, and bring the answer of their Great Father and all he said about them. "Then," said they, "we will go back with you and talk with him face to face." My "brother" told me to ascend the Red River in the Fall, and I should find the nation not far from the three big mounds near the head of that river, by which I suppose he meant some spurs of the Rocky mountains. "And when you reach these mounds," said he, "you will see the smoke from the grass that we will burn every day so that you may find us. You can come with but two men and you shall be safe. I will speak of you to all the Camanches, and tell them you are my brother: and none will hurt you. You can travel without fear through all our country; no one will dare to injure you or take your property." At parting with the Chiefs, they all embraced me most affectionately. My "brother," especially, showed all the feeling of a real brother; he threw his arms around my neck and burst into tears. Alasarea, the Towash, came to me last, and sat down with a grave and serious countenance. He several times struck his breast and said his heart was troubled. On my asking him the cause of his trouble, he said "when you came here, you had twenty-three men and now you have but twenty-two; one is dead. You say he was a good man." Yes, said I, he was a very good man. "You do not know how he was killed." No, I do not, but perhaps I shall know one day. "Many Camanches," said he, "are bad; many Quampas are bad; many of the Arripahoes are bad; many Towashes are bad, and so are many Pawnees. Some of all these are bad and they all hunt in this country. They might have killed the white haired man. He might have wounded a buffalo and been killed by him. A rattlesnake might have bit him. He is dead and you know not how. Here is my war horse Checoba. I give him to you: no horse among the Camanches will catch him. He will carry you away from every enemy and out of any danger." With this he led up a splendid black horse, worthy and fit to have borne a Richard Cœur De Leon, or a Saladin, into their greatest battles. No Arab could ever boast a finer animal than this; the finest limbed, the best proportioned, the swiftest and the most beautiful I ever saw. I brought him home, but before leaving the wilderness, his speed was greatly impaired by the bite of a rattlesnake.

CHAPTER VII

We start for home—A *stampedo*—Loss of a hundred horses—Interview with a Chief and his tribe—Pursued by Indians—Passage through the Cross Timbers—Death of horses by flies—Night travelling—Arrival at the Arkansas—Death of horses by the Feresy—Loss of skins and robes by embezzlement—Start for home—Breakfast with a Cherokee Chief—James Rogers—An old Cherokee—Interview with Missionaries—Arrival at home—Troubles from debt—An emergence at last—Conclusion.

AFTER PARTING with these simple children of nature, we prepared for our departure homeward. On the next day after packing up the goods, we abandoned the Fort and began to descend the river in perogues and by land, with the horses. Those in the boats who started before the others with the horses, were to stop at the unfinished Fort one hundred miles below, and there await them. I travelled by land with the horses and met with no occurrence worth mentioning till the second day. Then commenced a series of misfortunes and unavoidable accidents, which continued till I reached the settlements, and which destroyed all hope of profit from the adventure, and the consequences of which, have weighed upon me to this day with a crushing weight. As we travelled along the north bank of the river, a small herd of buffalo suddenly rushed out from the river bank on our left, before the horses and frightened many of them into a *stampedo* as the Spaniards call the thundering sound of their stamping, flying hoofs on the prairie. A few of the men rode after them and succeeded in turning them back; but their

152

shouts and use of the whips gave them another fright and they returned in a stampede among the drove, and thus spread the panic among them. About one hundred ran off at a furious rate, on the route of the river by which we had come. Placing the best rider in my company on Checoba, I ordered him to try his best speed and bottom in the pursuit. He started and ran sixteen miles, where he headed the flying horses that had become mingled with a wild drove, and he was driving them all before him and Checoba, when a rattlesnake bit the noble animal on the fore foot. Checoba immediately sickened and was brought back with great difficulty. On the following morning his foot and leg were swelled, and he was very lame and weak. I placed him in mud and water where he stood for several hours, when the swelling subsided and he was much relieved. By this accident I lost all the horses which ran off in the *stampedo,* and Checoba was materially injured for life. I remained till the next morning, when Checoba was able to travel, and I started with him in advance of the company. Soon after crossing a small branch, I saw an Indian about two hundred yards ahead in the prairie, who riding onto a high mound, hailed me with the word Tabbaho? As I replied, yes. I perceived several Indians approaching me from the prairie and my company behind, also observed them. McKnight and Adams hastened to reach me before the Indians, who came up friendly, and spoke to us in the Spanish language. As we three spoke Spanish, they took us for Spaniards, and said that they were of the Caddo tribe, who were in alliance with the Camanches. Some of the latter tribe and a number of Towashes were in their party, which they said was on its march behind them. They had just come out of a battle with the Osages, by whom they had been defeated, and were proceeding to tell us of the battle when I observed a party of about two hundred

Indians coming towards us and also noticed a small grove a short distance before us. I ordered my party to hasten forward to this grove and occupy it in advance of the Indians. As they drove the horses forward, the rope which held the pack on a horse, which I had brought from home with me, got loose and was trod on by the horses behind, which pulled the pack under his belly. He started forward, kicking and pitching until he had got rid of his load, and then returned at full speed among the drove, which broke into another stampede. Off they flew, and many of them ran entirely out of sight on the level prairie, with the speed of birds on the wing. I lost about thirty in this flight. We reached the grove at the same time with the Indians, who then discovered us to be Americans and not Spaniards, which greatly displeased some. The Chief, however, was friendly. An Indian took up and examined McKnight's gun, which he had left leaning against a tree, and riding into the crowd, brandished it over his head, exclaiming that we had stolen the horses; that they ought to take them from us and kill us. The old Chief ordered him to be silent, and he said if they would not kill us he would go and bring men who would do so, and started off in a gallop towards the Canadian with McKnight's gun. Many of the Indians charged us with having stolen Checoba from Alasarea the Towash, and seemed to believe the charge, and to consider us thieves who had been preying upon their countrymen. One who appeared to be the most blood thirsty, shot an arrow into the side of one of their own horses near the lights. The horse bounded forward and fell dead. This act excited them to the highest pitch, and the old Chief had great difficulty in protecting us from an attack; by an harangue and a decisive course he at length assuaged their animosity and excitement. Their late defeat by the Osages had embittered their minds, and pre-disposed them to view us with suspicion. Seven men among them carried wounds received in the late battle, and by request of the Chief I dressed these wounds with salve and sticking plaster. While I was thus engaged, I sent the men forward a short distance, when they awaited me with their rifles ready to return the fire of the Indians. But they parted with us peaceably, and the Chief with great cordiality entreated me to return to his country and trade with his tribe. We want, said he, the friendship and trade of the Americans. I always observed that the most sagacious and far-seeing of the Camanche Chieftains sincerely desired the friendship and alliance of the Americans. A proper course towards them will make them our fast friends and most valuable allies. An opposite one will render them most deadly and dangerous enemies, and especially so in the event of a war with England. A course of justice, fairness and liberality is the only judicious one; and in dealing with them, the greatest tact and much knowledge of Indian character is requisite for success in gaining their confidence and securing their lasting esteem and friendship. The Pawnees and all the tribes west of the Osages, called by the national name of Camanches, are all of the same original tribe, though bearing various names, and all speak the same language. They are in the strictest alliance with each other, and could probably muster a force of forty or fifty thousand warriors at the time I was among them. The United States should provide against the consequences of their hostility.

After parting from the Caddo Chief, I sent the company with the horses forward, and remained behind with McKnight to watch against pursuit by the Indians. Finding that we were not followed, we hastened on and overtook the rest of the company, and all reached the unfinished Fort in the afternoon, where we found the perogues and swivel in charge of the men who had brought them down the river and were awaiting us according to arrangement. We travelled on in company till night fall, when the land party crossed the river at a bend and encamped with the others in a grove. We carefully secured our horses. On the following morning, as we issued from the timber into the prairie, a dead buffalo cow was seen with her calf standing near her. We soon saw another cow lately killed by a party evidently in pursuit of us. We travelled in company with the perogues, that we might have the benefit of the swivel in case of an attack. In the Cross Timbers, which we reached in four or five days after leaving the last mentioned Fort; we again parted company with the perogues and struck out into the prairie. Here we soon afterwards observed a herd of buffalo running rapidly with their tongues hanging out of their mouths, and also, eight Indians mounted, who did not perceive us. In three days we passed the Cross Timbers and reached the long-grass prairies on the east of them. Here the horse flies were so numerous and ravenous as nearly to destroy the horses which were frequently covered entirely by them. Many of the horses died and all were wasting away under the inflictions of these venomous insects. To avoid them, we travelled only by night and slept by day. I took the direction by guess and in eight days, or rather, nights, we struck the Arkansas just five miles below the three forks, where Fort Gibson now stands, and the point which I was aiming to reach. I went up to the forks where Barbour's trading establishment was then situated and there obtained a canoe. Barbour, I afterwards learned, had died in New Orleans, whither he started with my keel boat on my outward trip. We travelled down the Arkansas to the mouth of the Canadian, and found the rest of my company with the perogues, awaiting us at the Salt works. Here I took an account of my stock, and found that out of three hundred and twenty-three horses and mules which I had purchased of the Indians and started with for home, I had lost by flies and *stampedos,* just two hundred and fifty-three, leaving but seventy-one now in my possession. These I allowed to rest one day, and on the next day lost five of them by a disease called the Feresy, which causes a swelling of the breast and belly and generally terminates fatally. On the day and night following, eight or ten more of the horses died and about twenty were sick with the disease. I was too anxious for my family and too desirous of seeing them to delay my departure any longer. Here, at the mouth of the Illinois River, a branch of the Arkansas, and near the mouth of the Canadian, I left the few horses and mules remaining, and the perogue containing the skins and robes, in charge of Adams & Denison. I never saw them again and lost all—horses and mules, beaver skins and buffalo robes. I returned home with five horses; just the same number I had started out with. Most of them died, and those that lived were never accounted for to me. The skins and robes were sold by James Adams, at *Eau-Post,* in Arkansas, on the river of that name, and the whole proceeds, amounting to a large sum of my money, were embezzled by him, the said Adams. He had been employed by McKnight and was unknown to me. In every respect, pecuniarily and otherwise, this was a most unfortunate venture. I lost by it my best and dearest friend, John McKnight, and all the money I had invested in it, with the vain hope of being thereby set free from debt and made an independent man. The object was a great one, and the risk proportionably great. I lost all that I had set upon the stake and was still more deeply involved than before. A dreary future lay ahead, but I determined to meet and struggle with it like a man.

Leaving the river, in company with twelve men, some afoot and some with horses, we directed our course for the Cherokee country. We found no game and for several days all suffered severely from hunger. We at length approached the Cherokee settlements; and I went forward alone promising the men to have a meal prepared for them at the house of John Rogers, a half breed Cherokee Chief. When in sight of his place I met Rogers and told him I wanted breakfast for myself and twelve men; that I had been among the Camanches trading, and that my company was coming up nearly starved. He replied that his tribe had been at war that year, with the Osages and had raised but a small crop, and that he had to pay one dollar per bushel for his bread "But," said he, "I will get you something to eat," and entering his house, requested his wife to prepare breakfast for twelve men, and with a smile, "twelve hungry men at that." I noticed in his house, all the usual furniture of our best farmers, and he was evidently living well and comfortably. The men came up, and by their rough exteriors, long beards and hair, lantern jaws and lank bodies, they strongly impressed me with the idea of a gang of famished wolves. They glared at Mrs. Rogers, while she was getting their breakfast, like so many cannibals, and had she not been very quick in appeasing their appetites, I cannot swear but that they would have eaten her up. She, the good woman, squaw though she was, exerted herself in our behalf like an angel of mercy, and in a miraculously short time she set before us a noble meal of bacon, eggs, corn bread, milk and coffee; there was enough for us all and we arose filled, leaving some on the table, not from politeness but from inability to eat any more. Well Mr. Rogers, said I, what shall I pay you for our breakfast. "What," said he, laughing, "would be the use of charging men who have just come out of the woods and cannot possibly have any money." No, said I, I am not begging my way; I will pay you with goods that I have. I then drew out my stock and sold him twelve dollars' worth, after paying for our meal. The father and sister of Rogers now came in and talked with us some time. The father, who was a white man, said that his son John killed the first Indian at the battle of the Horse-shoe, where both served on the side of the Americans under Jackson. "The Creeks," said he, "always fight till death. It takes one Cherokee for every Creek, and of the whites a little more than one for one." Both father and son spoke in the highest terms of Gen. Jackson, as a man, a soldier and a commander.

I requested provisions to subsist us till we could get a supply, and obtained from him sufficient to carry us to Matthew Lyon's trading house at the Spadre. Below this is a large Missionary station, which we were informed was well supplied with flour and meat, of which a boat load for their use had lately arrived. "If you find the missionaries in good humor," said Mrs. Rogers, "and do not go on the Lord's Day, you will be able to get some provisions, but not without. I was down at the station last week on Saturday and staid over Sunday. A Cherokee woman came in on Sunday from Piney, twenty miles above on the river, with some chickens to buy some sugar and coffee for a poor woman who had been lately confined. I interpreted for the woman, and went to brother Vail and told him what the woman wanted. I don't deal with the females, said he; you must go to sister ――――. We went to the sister that brother Vail had named, and she told me that they neither bought nor sold on the Lord's Day. Then take the chickens as a gift said I, and give the woman what she wants. We neither give nor take on the Lord's Day, said she, and the poor woman had to go back with her chickens, and so I advise you not to go to the Missionaries on the Lord's Day." I could hardly believe that bigotry and fanaticism could go so far as this, until

I found by experience, when I reached the station, that their meanness was fully equal to all I had heard. We left the hospitable house of the Cherokee Chief with many thanks and proceeded on our way. At a short distance from the Spadre, I was riding alone in advance of the company, when I met a gentlemanly and intelligent half-breed Cherokee, of whom I enquired if I could procure provisions at that place. He said I could not, but invited me to alight and take breakfast with him. There are too many of us said I, twelve beside myself. This did not daunt him and he immediately extended his invitation to all, and the whole company accordingly entered his house and partook of an excellent breakfast, such as that which his brother had furnished us two days before. This man was James, the brother of John Rogers, and lived like him in comfort and elegance. His wife was a handsome half-breed, whom I presented with some articles of dress, against the wish of her husband, who refused all pay for our breakfast. He purchased of me goods to the amount of fiteen dollars and paid me the money for them. We passed the Spadre that morning, where I saw the grave of Matthew Lyon, a man who made a considerable figure in politics in the Alien and Sedition times of John Adams. "After life's fitful fever he sleeps well." At Piney I saw a number of Indians, and enquired of them for provisions. We are hungry said I, and have nothing to eat. A negro woman said they were starving themselves and could not help us to any thing. I told the man we should be compelled to fast until we reached Weber's or the Missionaries. An old Indian who stood behind me during this colloquy, caught hold of my arm as I started on, and with a sharp enquiring look into my eyes, exclaimed, "nothing! nothing to eat?" Nothing at all said I. Come with me said he. I followed him about one hundred yards up the bank of a creek where he turned

up a hollow and entered a cabin under the brow of a hill:
going to the chimney he took from within it a stick holding three pieces of bacon and gave me two of them. I
offered him money. "No, said he, I take no money, but
when you meet a hungry Cherokee share with him whatever you have, as I have shared with you." Such conduct
as this, thought I, is practical Christianity, call it by what
name you please. Parting with this warmhearted Indian,
we hastened on toward the Missionary station, which we
reached the next day. This was situated on the north side
of the river, and was composed of about one hundred
persons, old and young, who occupied some twenty buildings arranged in a square. Here we hoped to obtain a
full supply of provisions, being informed that one hundred
barrels of pork and one hundred and fifty barrels of flour
had lately arrived for the use of the Missionaries and their
families. Entering the town I enquired for and found the
head of the concern, named Vail, laid before him our
destitute condition and misfortunes in the Camanche
country, and asked him for provisions enough to last us
to the settlements on the Little Red, seventy miles below.
"Well, said he, I will speak to brother such a one about
it," and went away for that purpose. Another man soon
came up and asked me how much we wanted. I replied,
about one hundred pounds of flour and fifty of pork.
"Well I vow and declare, I don't know how we shall be
able to spare it; how much would you be willing to give?"
Any reasonable price said I; what do you ask? We are
suffering from hunger and must have provisions. He left
me, saying he would see brother Vail about it and I
waited an hour without seeing either of them. I then
searched out brother Vail and repeated my request for
provisions. He vowed and declared that he did not think
they had more than enough "to do them the year round."
I then asked for one half the quantity I had named be-

fore. "We have a very large family, and if we should get out we could not get any more from the settlements." I said that what little we wanted would not make more than one meal for his family, and he could easily procure a new supply to prevent any suffering. "Well, said he, what would you be willing to give?" Set your own price on your property, said I, and I will give it, as I cannot do without provisions. He then went away, saying he would see the others, naming them. Robert McKnight now came from the blacksmith's shop, where he had got his mule shod on the fore feet and had been charged for that service the sum of two dollars. We concluded that they knew the price of horse-shoes, if not of flour and pork. Again I sought out the "brethren," Vail and the other, reiterated to them our wants, and requested relief as before: the eternal question was again put, what would you be willing to give? Any thing that you choose to ask said I. "We do not think we can spare any provisions," said one. They were waiting for a bid, and I determined not to huckster with the canting hypocrites, nor gratify them by paying an outrageously exhorbitant price, which they were expecting to get from my necessities. Without further parley I left them and went up to the bakery of the Station, where some of my company were trying to get some bread. I offered to pay for whatever they could sell. "No, we can't sell any thing without brother Vail's permission. I offered to buy two or three bushels of fragments of bread, which I noticed on the table in a corner. "We use them in soups and for puddings and do not waste any thing." My men were now furious and ready to take possession of the bakery and divide it out among them. With great difficulty I restrained them from this act. I told them they would render us all infamous in the settlements as robbers of Missionaries, those holy men of God; that we should be regarded with horror by all, wherever we went, if we preyed upon these lamb-like and charitable christians. I told them we must go on and trust to Providence. "What!" said McKnight, "travel on without provisions when there are plenty of them here. I will have some if need be by force." I at length prevailed on them to start without committing any depredation. When leaving the town, I saw Vail at a distance, rode up to him asked, what are you doing here? "We are instructing the Indians in the Christian religion." I think, said I, you might learn some of the principles of your religion from the Indians themselves. An old Cherokee yesterday gave me two out of three pieces of meat which he had, and refused pay for them in money. He told me to do the same by a Cherokee should I meet one in want. Here you are afraid to put a price on your flour and meat for fear of not charging enough. You wish me to name an exhorbitant price. You wish to make the most out of me and you shall make nothing. He was saying that charity began at home, he must provide for his own household and so forth, as I left him in disgust with his meanness and hypocricy. We now left the river and bore eastwardly, and that evening killed a turkey, upon which we lived two days and a half, when we reached Little Red River, where we procured an excellent dinner, and a supply of food from a settler whose name I forget. This was the first meal we had eaten, sufficient to break our fasts, since we had left James Rogers' house, five days before.

From this place I hastened home without any occurrence of note. My family was sick when I arrived, and my creditors soon became more clamorous than ever: each endeavored to anticipate the others, and the executive officers of all the Courts, from the United States District Court down to those of Justices of the Peace, swarmed around me like insects in August. I gave up all my property, even the beds upon which my children were born, and after all was sold, though the officers supposed there was enough to satisfy the judgments against me, there yet remained a large amount still due. The whole is now paid: in the twenty years which have intervened, I discharged all my debts on account of these two expeditions of which the narration is now closed. I lost by them about the sum of twelve thousand dollars, and after all the hardships I had endured, found myself poorer than ever. The reader has been told how I incurred these losses, most of which were, perhaps, under the circumstances, to have been expected. I was the first American that ever went among the Camanches for the purpose of trading. Before my first trip among them, their name was unknown to our people: the Americans called them Pawnees and knew them only by that name. They were then wilder and more ignorant of our power than now, when they have probably learned that we do not all live in one village, and derived from their kindred tribe, the Pawnees, and other neighbors, a tolerably correct indea of our strenth and numbers. Traders would now run very little risk of the robberies which I suffered from them, and probably none at all of being killed in time of peace. The trade would now be profitable; equally so as when I was among them, and from the greater cheapness of goods a greater profit could be made, while the dangers would be far less. Were it not for advancing age, I should repeat the adventures, notwithstanding their unfortunate issues heretofore. Age, however, forbids any farther attempts to retrieve my fortune in this manner. I have been enabled through the real friendship of a brother to support my family and give my children the rudiments and foundation of an education; which, though not such as I would have given them had better fortune attended me, is sufficient, if properly improved, to enable them to go through the world with honor and usefulness. I have uni-

formly endeavored to instil in their minds principles of
integrity and republicanism; and for myself, to bequeath,
as the richest inheritance I could leave them, a good example and an unsullied name. With strong bodies and
habits of labor, with honor and intelligence, they will
succeed in a country of liberty and equal rights to all.
I have always been true to my country, and uniformly
studied to advance the interests of my countrymen in all
my transactions with the savages and Spaniards; and I
have my reward in the satisfaction derived from a con-
sciousness and patriotic discharge of duty on all occasions.
At the age of sixty-three, with broken health, I feel none
of the peevishness of age; I look forward cheerfully and
hopefully on the coming days, without

> Shuddering to feel their shadows o'er me creep,

and rejoice, in my decline, over the rise and glorious prospects of my country. I have the consolation of being able
to recall to my mind several manifestations of the confidence and esteem of my fellow-citizens, exerted towards
me at a time when the hand of misfortune bore heaviest
upon my head. They did me the honor, in eighteen hundred and twenty-five, of electing me General of the Second Brigade, First Division of the Militia of Illinois, an
office which I now hold. I was also elected, in the same
year, to represent the country of Monroe in the Legislature of Illinois, of which I was a member for two ses-
sions. I was appointed Post Master in the same county in
eighteen hundred and twenty-seven and have held the
appointment ever since.

I would mention my agency in the Black Hawk war of
eighteen hundred and thirty-two, in which I served as
Major, were it not a war in which no honor was gained
by any one; and the history of which, for the credit of
the country, ought never to be written.

These proofs of the esteem of my countrymen are gratifying and consoling amidst the difficulties which have so long weighed me down, and are evidence that a generous people will appreciate the intrinsic character of a man, independent of adventitious circumstances, the frowns or the favors of fortune.

THE END

Appendix A

JOURNAL

OF A VOYAGE from St. Louis, La. to the Mandan Village, under-taken by the St. Louis Missouri Fur Company, for the purpose of conducting Shehekeh the Mandan chief to his nation, and to establish trading houses on the head waters of the Missouri; by Doctor Thomas, Surgeon to the party.

On the 17th of May last [1809], we set out from St. Louis with ten barges and one hundred and sixty men, well equipped, among whom were a few Delawares and Shawonie's, employed for hunting. On the next day, we passed the beautiful village of St. Charles, being 18 miles by land, and about 36 by water from St. Louis; ascending to the river Gasconade, the country is very thickly settled, particularly in those spots called Boons settlement, and near the little village called Charette. I am informed that the territory of Louisiana is portioned out in six districts; St. Charles is the uppermost, comprehending that immense tract of country, west of the Mississippi, and north of the Missouri; the tide of emigration appear to direct itself to this highly favored spot, and indeed we are not surprised that the farmers of the U. States bend their attention this way, as every advantage both of soil and climate, render it preferable to Kentucky or Ohio.

From the Charrette village to the Osage river, we experienced nothing extraordinary; having agreed to wait here for the party, we took advantage of the delay, to saunter over the country; this place is said to be about 40 miles from the frontiers, altho there is a small village opposite its mouth, on the north side of the Missouri, in a beautiful rich prairie; the inhabitants consist of emigrants from below, principally french; these people raise a sufficiency of grain for the consumption of

167

the settlement, and employ the balance of their time in hunting and trading with the surrounding Indians. The Osage
river, situate on the south side, from its magnitude at the
mouth form an important appendage to this country; I was
informed that boats ascended to the old Indian villages about
100 miles up, it waters are pure, gentle and well tasted, its
banks discover to the naked eye the riches it possess; Iron
Ore of the best kind cover a great portion of its surface. Here
the botanist could enjoy a feast; the Savannas filled with in-
numerable plants pregnant with all the sweets the florist could
desire; the lovers of hunting could not fail of finding on this
river plenty of amusement, for I am sure, no place I have yet
seen can equal it for fish and wild fowl.

Mine river empty's itself into the Missouri, a few leagues
above, is navigable for small craft up to the salt works; there
are two establishments here, and I am informed that 200 kettles
are constantly employed in making salt, a gentleman who rode
over the country where these salt licks abound, say, that
10,000 kettles might be employed, as strong water springs are
numerous in every direction. On the 3d of June we were
visited by a hail storm, and to render the scene more dis-
agreeable, one of the hunters, John Stout, had his thumb blown
off, and his hand much lacerated by the bursting of my gun.

On the 28th, all of the boats having arrived, we set out, and
on the 8th, of July arrived at *Fort Osage,* which we saluted
by a discharge of several guns from our ordnance barges, and
was politely answered by an equal number from the Fort:
here we experienced many civilities from the gentlemen of the
garrison. This place appears to be the general rendezvous of
all the Missouri indians, their continual jars keep the commandant on the alert. Osages, Ottos, Mahas, Paunie, Canas,
Missouri, Souex, Sac, Fox, Ioway, all mingle together here,
and serve to render this quarter, a most discordant portion of
the continent.

July 11th, we all got ready for embarkation, having laid in
vegetables, &c. and bid adieu to the face of civilized life,
pushed on our way. The face of the country on each side of
the river, is so monotonous up to the river Plat that one days
journey would nearly give the history of everything worthy of
notice. The banks in general are low and an extreme rich, dark
loam cover the surface of all its borders, except where the

cliffs approach the water; in several places they put in on both
sides, so as to compress the river to the breadth of 25 or 30
yards; to these bluffs, vegetation is denied; having ascended
many without being gartified [gratified] with the sight of a
plant; however our toils have been often repaid by the dis-
covery of various petrifications, the bones of the Buffaloe, Elk,
Goat, with the various kinds of wood which grow in the
neighborhood, are found on the tops of these cliffs, completely
petrified, yet few are to be found in the low land.

The Cansas river on the south side, so called from a nation
of that name, who reside about 150 miles up this river, is about
40 miles from the garrison, this river is considerable, affording
a navigation for trading boats, up to the village. The Cansas
have been long with terror of the neighboring indians, their
temerity is hardly credible; a few weeks since a band of 100
warriors entered the Paunie village, or what is more generally
called, the Paunie Republic, and killed the principal chief and
his family, consisting of 16 souls; they were immediately pursued and upwards of 40 of them cut to pieces; these people
cannot be at peace with the white or red people; they rob
murder and destroy when opportunity offer, fortunately [?]
for their neighbors they are few in number, and their daily
outrages serve to lesson their number still more, their country
abound with game, particularly Beaver, Deer, Buffaloe, Elk,
Black bear &c. &c. and afford the Cansas (hardly less savage)
an abundance of food and raiment.

On the 29th July, we arrived at Messrs Crooks and M'Clelland's old hunting camp, we lodged in their house, these gentlemen had constructed comfortable quarters, the house having
3 rooms, when they occupied it, the Ottos and Paunies resorted
to them in great numbers.

August 1st. arrived at the river Platte on the south side.
Met with Mr. M'Clelland, waiting for the Ottos, whom he
expected in great numbers to trade with.

Mr. M'Clelland has weathered many storms in this life, and
it appears that each day seem to throw something bitter in his
cup; brave, generous, and kind, he meets the untutored indian
with the smile of complacency; or if the temerity of the savage
should exceed the bounds of honesty or approach, to menace:
then M'Clelland discovers his exaulted courage, surrounded
with indians, with his rifle, pistols &c., sword, he bids defiance

to whole nations; threatening or executing extermination on all who attempt to plunder him.

The river Platte is about a half a mile wide at its mouth, it has almost as many mouths as the Mississippi, having numerous sand bars at its junction with the Missouri, its waters has the muddy hue of the Missouri, its extreme rapidity and shoal water, prevent the traders ascending it; the Otto villages is about 40 miles from the mouth; the Paunies reside a considerable distance above and extend to near the head waters of the Arkansa, these people living in the neighborhood of the Spanish villages, near St. Fee, trade alternately with them and the American traders. These Parthians of the west ought to be cherished, as through them we may obtain an extensive trade with that portion of Mexico, most adjacent to the mines.

(to be continued)

[From the *Louisiana Gazette,* Thursday, November 30, 1809. The issues for December 2 (except for first page) and for December 14, 1809, are missing from the microfilm copy in the San Diego State College Library. I have been unable to locate copies of those issues. A. P. N.]

Appendix B

LETTER

Thomas James to President Andrew Jackson, February 21, 1834

To His Excellency Andrew Jackson
President of the United States of North America.

Your memorialist Thomas James of the county of Monroe State of Illinois shews to your Excellency that in the year 1821 he left this State with a large assortment of goods for the purpose of trading with the various tribes of Indians which inhabit the country between our western frontier and the settlements of New Mexico. That for that purpose he obtained from the Hon. Jno. Q. Adams, then Secretary of State a passport No. (57) dated 6th March 1821, under the seal of his office, which was countersigned by Don Francisco Dionisso Vivès his Catholic majesty's minister of Spain to the U. States as well as license by Robt. Crittenden the then acting governor of the Territory of Arkansas, to trade with the various tribes of Indians that inhabit the Arkansas river and its tributary streams, having previously entered into bond for the faithful observance of the Laws of the United States regulating the trading with the Indians.

In the prosecution of this enterprise he traversed the country inhabited by the Comanche Indians who claim a large country within the limits of the Territory of the United States. This tribe are very numerous and warlike can assemble six or eight thousand warriors about sixteen thousand horses and mules. Their horses are perhaps superior to any in the United States. They inhabit the country on both sides of the line, spending about half their time on each side of the line. They lead a wandering life regulating their movements by the direction that the buffaloe herds takes from north to south.

Your memorialist was plundered by these Indians of ten thousand dollars worth of goods being the greater part of the stock he had with him. They continued to follow him to Santa Fe, in New Mexico. At that place in 1822 they informed him that if he would return and trade with them, he should not be molested. That they were anxious to have traders from the United States and form an alliance with the Americans. Accordingly your memorialist returned with goods in 1823 and 1824 and traded with them, would have made a profitable adventure, had not a renewal of Hostilities have taken place between them and the Osage Indians. During this Expedition in council with these Indians they informed him that they were anxious to go and see the president and become friendly. That they were not and would not be under the protection of the Spanish government. That the United States had made treaties with the Osages, Pawness and Sious, had furnished them with agents, traders, and armourers, that they had none, and proposed coming with your memorialist to see the American father. They further stated that if the president would treat with them that your memorialist might return with but two men or alone and they would go to any place with him to make a treaty. That if the United States would do so, would furnish them an agent and traders, that they would act in good faith toward them. They ask for protection against the Osages and other Indians at amnity [*sic*] with our government. They stated that the Santa Fe trade should not be molested, and that they would protect the Americans, that the Spaniards had not the articles they wished to trade for and strongly desired your memorialist to return authorized to make a treaty with them. That in that event they would pay him for the property of which they had plundered him. These facts were communicated to Hon. Dan. P. Cook and then representative from this state in Congress, but believed never to have been acted on.

Your memorialist respectfully prays your Excellency to authorize him or some other person or persons to treat for the government with these Indians. From his knowledge of the country they inhabit, their numbers and resources, the security it would give to the frontier, to the traders and enterprising citizens of the United States. Advantageous so highly to the welfare and prosperity of a numerous set of enterprising and useful citizens and doing justice to the undersigned who has lost his all, could not fail but be productive of the most happy results.

Respectfully your fellow citizen and friend

THOMAS JAMES

The undersigned are and have been for a long time acquainted with General Thomas James and we take great pleasure in testifying to his character as being every way unexceptionable. That he sustains an irreproachable character for Probity and Honor and stands high with his fellow citizens. He has ever been a firm and devoted friend to the present administration and is in every way a worthy subject of government patronage. We would recommend him as well qualified for the agency spoken of or any other in the gift of the government.

St. Clair County Illinois
21 February 1834

A. W. SNYDER
Senator
St. Clair County
Illinois
WILLIAM KINNEY
JOHN HAY

Your excellency will please refer to Misters Kane, Robinson, Casey, Slade and Duncan of Illinois for further particulars in relation to my claims for the appointment or any other in that line. I have thought it unnecessary to procure other names to the above having procured three tried friends of your Excellency who are advantageously known.

T. James.

[National Archives, Records of the Office of Indian Affairs, *Pawnee*, 1834. Printed in Missouri Historical Society *Bulletin*, X, 87-89.]

KEYSTONE BOOKS

Keystone Western Americana

THE LEWIS AND CLARK EXPEDITION by Meriwether Lewis (3 vols.) (KB-34, -35, -36)

ASTORIA by Washington Irving (2 vols.) (KB-37, -38)

COMMERCE OF THE PRAIRIES by Josiah Gregg (2 vols.) (KB-52, -53)

MOUNTAINS AND MOLEHILLS by Frank Marryat (KB-49)

THE PERSONAL NARRATIVE OF JAMES O. PATTIE (KB-50)

THREE YEARS AMONG THE INDIANS AND MEXICANS by Thomas James (KB-51)

Keystone Short Stories

COLOR OF DARKNESS by James Purdy (KB-25)

THE GAMES OF NIGHT by Stig Dagerman (KB-26)

THE DIGNITY OF NIGHT by Klaus Roehler (KB-27)

WHITE APPLES by Arno Karlen (KB-29)

THE SWING by Vera Cacciatore (KB-30)

THE GO-AWAY BIRD by Muriel Spark (KB-31)

TELL ME A RIDDLE by Tillie Olsen (KB-32)

THE END OF PITY by Robie Macauley (KB-39)

THE LAST HUSBAND by William Humphrey (KB-40)

HAPPY FAMILIES ARE ALL ALIKE by Peter Taylor (KB-41)

NEW WORLD WRITING 16 (KB-17)

NEW WORLD WRITING 17 (KB-20)

NEW WORLD WRITING 18 (KB-24)

NEW WORLD WRITING 19 (KB-33)

NEW WORLD WRITING 20 (KB-42)

THE ART OF MAKING SENSE by Lionel Ruby (KB-15)
MORE IN ANGER by Marya Mannes (KB-16)
THE ART SPIRIT by Robert Henri (KB-18)
GUY DOMVILLE by Henry James (with biographical chapters by
Leon Edel) (KB-19)
RELIGION AND THE MODERN MIND by W. T. Stace (KB-21)
THE PICARESQUE SAINT by R. W. B. Lewis (KB-28)
POETRY AND MATHEMATICS by Scott Buchanan (KB-43)
THE PILGRIMAGE OF WESTERN MAN by Stringfellow Barr (KB-45)

Keystone Discographies

THE COLLECTOR'S BACH by Nathan Broder (KB-3)
THE COLLECTOR'S JAZZ: *Traditional and Swing* by John S. Wilson
(KB-4)
THE COLLECTOR'S HAYDN by C. G. Burke (KB-7)
THE COLLECTOR'S CHOPIN AND SCHUMANN by Harold C. Schon-
berg (KB-8)
THE COLLECTOR'S TCHAIKOVSKY AND THE FIVE by John Briggs
(KB-9)
THE COLLECTOR'S JAZZ: *Modern* by John S. Wilson (KB-10)
THE COLLECTOR'S TWENTIETH-CENTURY MUSIC IN THE WESTERN
HEMISPHERE by Arthur Cohn (KB-23)
THE COLLECTOR'S VERDI AND PUCCINI by Max de Schauensee
(KB-46)
THE COLLECTOR'S BEETHOVEN by John Briggs (KB-47)

Keystone Books in Medicine

EPILEPSY: *What It Is and What to Do About It* by Tracy J.
Putnam, M.D. (KB-1)
LIVING WITH YOUR ALLERGY by Samuel M. Feinberg, M.D.
(KB-2)
HELP FOR TEN MILLION: *Arthritis, Rheumatism and Gout* by
Darrell C. Crain, M.D. (KB-5)
CATHARTICS AND COMMON SENSE by William Farrar, M.D.
(KB-6)
HEARING LOSS by Greydon G. Boyd, M.D. (KB-11)
HIGH BLOOD PRESSURE by Eugene B. Mozes, M.D. (KB-12)
PARKINSON'S DISEASE by Lewis J. Doshay, M.D. (KB-13)
WILL MY HEART FAIL? by William A. Jeffers, M.D. (KB-14)
YOU AND YOURS: *How to Help Older People* by Julietta K.
Arthur (KB-22)